I0027003

NIQQIE AND CHARCOAL + RUTH ANN
WRITTEN BY DR. CAL

COLLABORATION AND CRITICAL REVIEW BY
<u>MEGAN SHORT</u>

A NOVEL BASED ON REAL LIFE

DURING THE 1970s, 80s, and 90s in most urban neighborhoods in the United States, then and now.

This novel is released, <u>accompanied</u> by 1980s hip hop musical video & booklet of verses designed to counsel and treat active drug and sex addiction. It is titled,
"HIP HOP RYHMES OF TOUGH LOVE TO ADDICTS, OUT OF CONTROL";
"<u>A 7 Minute Treatment</u>". ($10.99)

HARD BOUND ($19.99) PRINTED BY SHERIDAN BOOKS, VIDEO by MOSCAL ($11.99) NOVEL AND HIP HOP VIDEO AS A PACKAGE MUST BE ORDERED DIRECTLY FROM PUBLISHER AND PAID THROUGH @PayPal account: Discounted package price ($27.99) MOSCAL PRODUCTION & PUBLISHING; P.O. Box 470618, L. A. CA., 90047, ph. 424-702-5210

PAPERBACK COPIES ($11.99) PRINTED & DISTRIBUTED BY CREATESPACE.COM AND KDP-SUPPORT@AMAZON.COM

****

This novel is
A PROGRESSIVE ST0RY OF
DRUG ADDICTION AND SEX ADDICTION

Also exposes the color discrimination practiced between light skin and dark skin black Americans.

(Disclaimer): The story, names of the characters in this novel are fictitious; THE SEXUAL BEHAVIOR OF PERSONS IN THIS NOVEL MAY NOT BE SUITABLE READING FOR CHILDREN)

This novel is based on real life experiences that may be observed in some behavior of some addicts and some ordinary people throughout America as researched by this Author. **SEXUAL BEHAVIOR, CIRCUMSTANCES AND ADULTS IN THIS NOVEL ARE REAL, BUT HAS BEEN REVISED IN WORDS, SYNCHRONIZED, AND MAY BE DEEMED FICTITIOUS. THE SEXUAL RENDITION OF AND BY CHARACTERS MAY NOT BE SUITABLE READING FOR CHILDREN)**

ALL CHARATERS IN THIS NOVEL ARE FICTICIOUS

CHARACTERS:

1. Kashimba Seberg (Kashi) boy left alone in apartment)

2. Monique Ann Nazareth Seberg (Wife), Niqqie, mother of boy left alone),

3. Charcoal (Malcolm Jacob Seberg (husband)

4. Ruth Ann Nazareth (mother of Niqqie),

5. Melba (friend of Niqqie)

6. Thomas Joe Seberg (Father of Charcoal),

7. Roberta May Seberg (Mother of Charcoal)

8. Melba (old friend of Niqqie),

9. Tom Joubert (White father of Niqqie)

10. Margaret (Maggie) Rosenberg Joubert (white wife of Tom Joubert)

11. Tara (daughter of Tom and Margaret),

12. Sawyer (son of Tom and Margaret)

13. Terry (Midwife at abortion clinic)

14. Josie Antoinette Maldonado (moderator at AA meeting)

14. Corrina Bea Scott (friend introducing Niqqie at AA meeting)

15. Chelsea (jealous black girl at AA meeting)

16. Mavis (male at AA meeting)

17 Flyboy (Drug pusher supplying Charcoal)

18 Connie (Niqqie's job supervisor)

19 Toni (Niqqie's girlfriend in drug house)

20 Maniac (Pusher who raped Niqqie)

21. Teeki (homosexual friend of Charcoal)

22. Sergeant Kato (black policeman taking Kashi)

23. Chris (drug house owner)

24. Tripolie (wife of drug house owner)

This novel is based on real life experiences that may be observed in behavior of addicts and some ordinary people throughout America, as researched by this Author. **SEXUAL BEHAVIOR OF ADULTS IN THIS NOVEL IS TRUE, BUT HAS BEEN REVISED IN WORDS AND SYNCHRONIZED, AND MAY BE DEEMED FICTICTITOUS. THE SEXUAL RENDITION OF AND BY CHARACTERS MAY NOT BE SUITABLE READING FOR CHILDREN)**

INTRODUCTION:

The title, "Niqqie and Charcoal + Ruth Ann", is created. All the names of characters in this novel are fictitious.

Many stories have been written about drug addiction. Many movies have been shown to depict drug and sex addictive behavior.

This novel, however, takes you the reader into the drug house and reveals how the drug mind controls the actual sex behavior at the time the sex is being performed, and the role it plays in the addiction scenario. This novel crystallizes what constitutes sex addiction by explaining and defining nymphomania (sex addiction) in women, in chapter 15.

This novel also explains how a male is turned out in childhood to become homosexual and vividly demonstrated in chapter 12.

This novel demonstrates the psychological addiction process of sex addiction and drug addiction that takes place in the mind of a person before, during, and after one has been addicted to drugs in chapter 14. You the reader will be taught and entertained by reading this novel.

The storyline of this novel has been synchronized to show continuity based upon real experiences. My research through content analysis, Behavioral Science, Social Science, as a Specialist in Child & Adolescent Psychotherapy, Historian, Family Head, Christian Counselor, Social Worker, Drug Counselor, Teacher.

The opening chapter emphasizes why child abuse is engaged in among drug addicts. Drug addicts with children are emphasized in this first chapter, because it is the most tragic outcome by all kinds of addicts.

In the next part of this novel (chapter 10), some scenes demonstrate the vulnerability of women who are turned out by addictive partners to be sex addicts demonstrated, when a woman has become addicted to addictive drugs and Alcohol, as explained in drug sex scenarios. Sex addiction may drive some into prostitution as seen in one case cited in this novel on pages 102-103. Drug and Sex addiction may also provoke homosexual behavior as seen in the case of Charcoal the husband of Niqqie.

Some chapters (chapter 6) illustrates the truism of color and racial intra-discrimination among Black Americans. This is illustrated in the lives of the titled characters. As such, sex and drug addiction becomes a driving force used in maintaining a sexual lifestyle. That, coupled with the continual use of the drug of choice, creates an addictive scenario. In the last part of this novel that begins with the chapter **Relapse,** "Alcoholics Anonymous" meetings becomes a teaching tool to all of this novel's readers.

CHAPTER 1

KASHI, LEFT ALONE; TAKEN TO JUVINILE HALL

Kashimba (Kashi as he is called) pulled the chair close to the window.
It was his dad's chair.

He had been told many times not to sit, stand or lie in that chair.
It seemed that every time Kashimba got near that chair, his mother would scream;
"Get out of that chair boy! You know your daddy would kill you if he found you in that chair!"

His mother would rush over, brutally grab him, and throw him across the room.
Kashimba would sit frightened for awhile.

His big round eyes glistened like two pools of milk with an Oreo cookie in the middle.
Tears wet his hands which were clenched tightly due to fear and rage.

Fear, because he knew his Mother would hurt him;
Rage, because he was not allowed to sit in that chair.

Kashimba did not see any reason why he was not allowed to sit in that velvety chair.

Finally, he maneuvered the chair just under the window so he could see the street from his second story window.

As he pulled the chair along, it got caught in the rug and almost tipped over.
The cushion was loosened as the chair tipped.

As he prepared to sit down, Kashi noticed something sticking out of the corner where the cushion had come loose.

He began to think to himself.
"It's a little pipe just like the one daddy and mommy smoke from.

Umm, it has that same funny smell that makes me sick when mommy and daddy smoke it. They think I am asleep and don't know what they are doing, but I do.

My friend from down the hall said her mommy smokes weed and a pipe too.
She feels good when she smells the smoke; but her mommy makes her leave the room.
Lateka said she feels good when she drinks from her mommy's glass of beer and I should try it.

My daddy sucks from the pipe like this".

Kashima sucked on the pipe long and hard, until he felt faint.

As Kashi mouthed the pipe, he thought of food and remembered that he was hungry.
He had not eaten all day.

His daddy left two days ago and his mommy left that morning to look for daddy.

Kashimba was six years old on his last birthday and he was trying to be a grownup.
His clothes hung loosely over his slender body, as though they were too big for him.

The shadows of darkness were now prominent in his house,
And he sat alone trying not to be frightened, but to no avail.

As he fought back the tears, he wondered:

"Where is mommy, I did as she told me. I have not left the apartment.
I'm hungry; I could have eaten at school if she would have let me go.
She said she would be back with some food, but she has been gone all day.
I wonder where she is."

Kashi saw some men beginning to gather on the corner.

As he continued to stare at the men through the window, he heard,

"Look out, here they come again! Run!"

The screeching noise from the tires of the car was drowned out

by the "rat tat tat tat" of the gun as the car came into view.

Kashi hit the floor like a soldier in combat and crawled behind the couch,

Like he had been told to do.

Kashi's little body began to shake as though a vibrator was inside him.

One bullet pierced the window where Kashi had sat a second ago.

He began to cry profusely and screamed "Oh God! Mommy! Mommy!"

People were screaming, and then the noise stopped as

Suddenly as it had started.

He heard the screeching of tires as the car pulled away.

Then Kashi heard the usual sound of sirens wailing as police and ambulances arrived

at the scene.

Kashi crawled out from behind the couch and made his way to

The door. Easing the door open, he saw people beginning to gather in the hallway.

One lady said, "Some people have been shot, where is your mother Kashi?"

Kashi shrugged and said, "I don't know."

The lady asked,

"Are you by yourself Kashi?"

Before Kashi could answer, the police came into the hallway.

The lady said,

"Get back in the house quick," as she ran back to her

Apartment and closed the door.

Soon, there was a knock on Kashi's door, but he did not answer.

Kashi had been told not to answer the door by his parents.

The knock sounded again and Kashi heard a voice say,

"Hello, are you in there? This is the police. Don't be afraid, we want to

talk to you. Open the door."

Kashi answered, "My mother is not home and I'm not supposed to open the door."

The police began to bang on the door real hard, saying;

"Open this door boy or we will break it down."

Kashi became panic-stricken and was crying loudly by now.

"My mommy ain't home" cried Kashi.

"Open this door boy or we are going to break it down right now!"

When Kashi heard a loud crash against the door, Kashi said,

"I'm coming."

Kashi open the door and tried to run past the police.

A white policeman grabbed him by the arm and picked him up, and shook him saying;

"Don't you run away from me boy."

He harshly carried him back into the apartment and slammed him onto the couch.

Kashi was screaming all the while, because he was frightened,

And the policeman was hurting his arm.

Kashi was beginning to feel rage building up inside him.

Kashi had been told, and everybody knew, white policemen wanted to hurt black

Men.

Kashi continued to sob and would not answer any of the

Policeman's questions.

Finally, Sergeant Kato the black policeman in charge said,

"Go next door and ask that lady, whom Kashi called Aunt Melba, to

come and try to quiet this boy down".

Melba came and hugged Kashi. After which, Kashi quieted down.

After that, the black Policeman in charge explained to Melba about
the mandatory reporting law the police operated under. He said:

"California law is very specific about agencies such as police, welfare, schools and others who serve the public. Such agencies are legally responsible to report, in due time, any alleged child abuse or elder abuse".

The Officer called Sergeant Kato told Melba,

"Children's Services will be called and
a Social Worker will be waiting at the station to interview and
take Kashi to Juvenile Hall".

Melba said,
"That will not be necessary, I always keep Kashi when Monique and Charcoal leaves. Come here baby."

"Charcoal?" the other Black policeman said,
"Is that the black nigger that thinks he's smart? Man, he and his old lady are two of the worst crack heads in the hood; I started to whip his head the other day."
Another policeman said in an undertone, "yeah, but, she's that sexy
Pretty little thing".

Sergeant Kato the Black policeman in charge continued: "Is this his boy?"

Melba nodded, in agreement.

"Ma'am, I can't let you take this responsibility, we have to take this child,
and anyway, taking this beautiful child may shock his parents to their senses.

Its people like you, who are enablers who want to help the drug addicts, who may be a
good friend, but, keep our people using drugs, and participating in gang activities?

You may think you're helping them, when all you're doing, is giving them greater
opportunities to continue to violate the law and hurt our own people."

"What has happened here today", he continued,

"Is a violation of the law? Kashi's parents may not have been
involved in the shooting, but they have violated the Child
Abuse and Child Neglect laws by putting their child in certain and constant danger.

Suppose that bullet that's lodged in the wall over there from the shooting,
Would have hit this child;

His mother and father would have been in real deep trouble.
Now, do you understand"?

Melba nodded in agreement.

The police Sergeant continued,

"The Law states that any parent is guilty of severe neglect;

When they willfully cause, or permit a child to be placed in a situation

where there is a clear and present danger to the child's person, and or health, including

the intentional failure to provide adequate food, clothing, shelter, or medical care.

Do you understand that"?

Melba again nodded in agreement.

"Now, do you still want to claim you were taking care of Kashi"?

Melba shook her head in a negative way.

Tears flowed from Melba's eyes, because she knew the
Policeman was right.

She watched Kashi in the police car until the car rounded the corner.

After they were out of sight, the image of
Kashi in the police car continued to flash back into her mind.

Melba immediately sent someone to find Niqqie to tell her that
 Kashi had been taken by the police.

Melba was saddened because Kashi was now confiscated by the court system and will become a child of the system.

Melba knew what that meant. She knew that Kashi's father Charcoal too, was confiscated and became a product of the court system.

Kashima was taken to the police station. He was later picked up and taken to Los Angeles County Juvenile Hall.

He is now sitting alone in the lobby of the intake room of the juvenile facility.

He was taken to the facility by the Children's Social Worker after she picked him up from the police station.

In the 1970s and 1980s, this facility was known as Mac McLaren Hall in Los Angeles County and was used to temporarily keep children of all ages brought in from the field. The children were housed until sent to jail, or given back to their parents at home, or placed in foster care, or group homes. But, only as the Superior Court of Los Angeles County ordered.

The Court used Licensed Social Workers, licensed and trained as Child Abuse Investigators, to prepare and present each case to the Court's Attorney.

This kind of facility is used by the courts to process cases of abused, abandoned, or neglected children.

Many of these children are not returned to their parents, but go on to

Become wards of the court and put in foster care, group homes, or sent to jail.

Kashi heard the desk clerk tell someone, it was two A.M. in the morning.

Normally, he would be asleep, but Kashi was wide awake.

He had been given a sandwich while waiting at the police station for the social worker,

but he was still hungry.

Kashi thought of how his mother would hold him when he

Became frightened. She would wrap her arms all the way

Around him and squeeze and rock him from side to side.

In her softness, Kashi felt warm and secure. How Kashi longed for

that feeling now.

The night worker named Jake, and the night supervisor, whose name is Hilda, came

over to him.

The night worker introduced Kashi to the night Supervisor.

The Supervisor said, "Are you ready to go to bed now Kashi?"

Kashi said, "No, I'm hungry."

The supervisor said, "Oh! I'm sorry Kashi; I didn't know you hadn't eaten."

After consulting with the night worker, the Supervisor of the unit

Leaned over and said to Kashi, "How about us settling for a big apple,

And tomorrow when you get up, you can have as much as you

Want for breakfast."

Kashi nodded his approval, and was taken to his bed.

CHAPTER 2

SOCIAL WORKER'S VISIT

The next day, Kashi's was assigned to the Social Worker name, Dr. Carrie Louise Sophisengberg, A beautiful, tall brown hair stately white woman, who spoke like she was raised in the ghetto?

In the meantime, while Kashi was being taken by the Police, Niqqie was getting high with drug buddies for the remainder of the night. Later, someone came and told Niqqie that Melba was looking for her.

The next day Niqqie drove her car back to her apartment as soon as she could get away from her drug buddies.

When she got home the next day, Melba told her the whole story. That is when Niqqie began to think about her present situation again.

"Now, my baby has been taken away from me, I might be evicted from my apartment, I might as well be dead."

Niqqie began to cry until she fell asleep from exhaustion from being out all night smoking crack cocaine.

Carrie the social worker was finally able to locate Niqqie through Melba and contacts in the community. The Social Worker arrived at Niqqie's apartment the

next day. She knocked on the door but nobody answered.

After a while, she went to the door and knocked again. She stood for a little while, and then went next door to Melba's place.

Melba told her that she thought Niqqie was home, because she had talked to her earlier. The Social Worker left a card with Melba and one in Niqqie's door.

The next morning when Niqqie awoke, she found the card the Social Worker had left there.

A slow invading panic began within her body, partly from her desire for crack cocaine and the anticipation of an interview with her social worker.

She knew that her welfare check would be stopped if she was not able to get the Social Worker to let her son come home.

The thought of her entire situation, aroused in her all the shame, guilt, and anger that anybody would want to experience.

The beauty of her once proud, dignified, and feminine self has been cascading downward since she first used crack cocaine. Her self esteem was in disrepair, and her body was only a shadow of what it once was.

In anticipation of the Social Worker's visit, Niqqie tried to make herself look better, but she was unable to fill in all the sagging facial skin and the tiredness she felt from being in constant pursuit of the u-topic high that only drugs like crack cocaine could produce. She took a shower, combed her hair and sat down to wait for the Social Worker.

The Social Worker returned to Niqqie's apartment and knocked on the door and Niqqie answered straight away. Niqqie opened the door and said, "Hello".

This time the Social Worker formally introduced herself.
"Are you Monique Ann Nazareth?"

Niqqie responded, "Yes I am".

"My name is, Dr. Carrie Louise Sophisengberg", and handed Niqqie her card.
She said, "please call me Carrie. I understand you are called Niqqie. May I call you Niqqie?"

Niqqie responded, "Yes".
Looking at the card, Niqqie said, "Oh, are you a Doctor"?

Carrie replied,
"No, I am not a Medical Doctor.

I am a Social Worker with a PhD in Children's Psychotherapy".

Niqqie said,
"Oh! are you going to be psychoanalyzing me, Carrie"?

Carrie responded with a question, "Is that what you want me to do"?

Niqqie responded, "I don't know, Doctor"!

The Social Worker took one look at the fine figure of a woman that is Niqqie, and said under her breath, "whoa"!

Carrie the Social Worker was immediately sexually aroused and attracted to Niqqie, because Carrie's is bi-sexual who fucked women as well as men.
Carrie spoke very quickly to distract her eye that was glued to the body of Niqqie.

They exchanged greetings of admiration. Niqqie offered Carrie the Social Worker, some coffee and she accepted.

Carrie soon found out that Kashi's mother, whose name is Monique, but everyone call her Niqqie, was a shapely, stunningly beautiful, young light skin black woman with a captivating smile and the personality to match. In other words, Niqqie was very desirable.

After more small talk, Carrie said to Niqqie,
"Are you Monique, kashi's mother?"

Niqqie said in a humble way,
"yes I am".

Carrie then said to Niqqie;

"I must inform you that everything we say here today is confidential. That means that anything you reveal about your personal life will be kept confidential and will not be revealed to anyone. But, you must be truthful and tell me everything. Do you understand what that means Niqqie?"

Niqqie responded as though Carrie was demeaning and talking down to her.
So she spoke sarcastically.

"Hell yes!! Of course I know what that means. I'm not a stupid ignorant young black girl just because I have a problem. I work for a contractor who supplies professional clerical staff to businesses and I do work on occasion for a law firm as a legal transcriber.
"Do you know what that means, Doctor!?"

Carrie relied
"Oh! I am glad you understand your rights. I am going to try and make that work for your benefit. May I finish now, Niqqie"?

Niqqie said, "Yes, go on".

The Social Worker said;
"let's begin with your real age and your real name. **Give me your driver's license**".

Niqqie handed the Social Worker her driver's license.

Carrie continued,
"Our conversation will be recorded. If you need me to stop the machine at any time, just

say so. Are you ready?" Niqqie started to cry again.

Carrie allowed Niqqie a chance to gather herself.

Then, Carrie spoke instantly,
"Why did you leave your son alone like that?"

Immediately, in a typical drug addict's usual attempt to lie, Niqqie began to stutter and try to explain that:
"I had gone to the corner store to get milk, and I was only gone for a short time".

Niqqie was displaying the typical drug addictive behavior of immediately lying to cover their drug behavior when they have been caught.

She pleaded for Kashi to be returned home.

She was told by the Social Worker.
"Monique, you have forfeited your right to keep Kashi at this time, when you left him alone. Now the court will decide in about four days where Kashi will live. I will also tell you what you will have to do before I let you see Kashi, or when Kashi can be returned to you. Kashi will remain as a ward of the Court in juvenile hall until he is returned to you, or placed in another location or placed in a Forster home for his well being.
In the meantime, I need to set up an appointment to sit down and talk to you. May I come by tomorrow please ".
Niqqie said yes, and arranged to meet with the social worker at Her apartment at 10:00 A.M. the next day.

Niqqie told the social worker to call on Melba's phone and gave her the number, Because her phone had been turned off. She thought, "Melba is a good friend and a soft shoulder to cry on and won't mind."

Chapter 3

NIQQIE THINKS BACK

After Carrie the Social Worker left Niqqie, Carrie was still fixated on Niqqie's body. As a bisexual woman, Carrie could not help but think about what it would be like to engage Niqqie in a sexual encounter.

Niqqie's mind however, was pre-occupied with her failings as a mother.

She said to herself,
"how did I get myself in this damn mess? I May not ever see my Kashi again."
Niqqie started to cry again.

She thought to herself;
"I gave Charcoal the hundred dollar bill my mother had given to Kashi. He took it, and didn't come back. I woke Kashi up, and told him I was going out to look for his daddy, and don't answer, or open the door for anybody, and don't go to school until I come back.

That was why Kashi was found alone during that gang shootout, and kashi was taken by the police and ended up in juvenile custody.

When I found Charcoal with his homosexual male friend, Teeki, they were freebasing my money away.

I joined them and forgot about my baby at home. That's why my baby was found alone and taken to juvenile hall.

If I hadn't left home that morning, I would still have my baby with me. That was the first drug crisis I went through. Now I must face my Social Worker and explain why I left Kashi alone.

"Damn! Damn!" Niqqie started to cry again.

The next day when the social worker arrived, Niqqie was up waiting for her.

She offered the social worker some coffee and the social worker accepted.

They exchanged some personal observations of each other.

Again, Carrie the Social Worker informed Niqqie that their conversation would be recorded and kept confidential.

My first Question, said Carrie:
"Were you born and raised in Los Angeles"? Carrie asked.

"Oh, that's a long story. Are you sure you want to hear about that?" Niqqie asked.

Carrie replied, "Yes, tell me everything"

Niqqie said she has wanted to tell someone about her life as her mother had told it to her for a long time.

Niqqie began this part of the story of her life by saying:

"My mother's name is, Ruth Ann Nazareth. We have been bonded together since my birth, and when you hear how I was conceived you will understand why.

My mother Ruth Ann named me, Monique Ann Nazareth". My last name, Nazareth, is the last name of my grandmother Lucy Ann Nazareth. She conceived my mother, Ruth Ann, while my grandmother was the maid and mistress of a prominent white man named, Shane Benedict Cavanaugh, who lived in a big house down near the Mississippi river in New Orleans Louisiana."

Carrie asked,

"Did his wife know he was having sex with Lucy Ann your grandmother"?

Niqqie replied:

"Oh, of course his wife knew about the sexual relations alright, because he was fucking Lucy Ann his house maid, and any of the black women who worked for the family, that would let him. That was common practice during those days, and their wives knew it.

He did not physically rape any of them, but his white male power over them, made them feel conducive.

Of course, his wife ignored and acted as though she didn't know anything about what her husband was doing.

All the black women in his employment had a lot of fun trying to avoid him. Some were able to avoid his grasp, but, others allowed him to have his way with them.

Fucking their maids by white Plantation owners, was a common practice in the south during and after slavery, and even after black slaves was freed. And it is still going on today".

"How do you think that some of the American Black race became so light skin or half white? It certainly wasn't because black men were freely fucking white women.

Most black women who were maids accepted their slave master's sexual advances, because;

First, they did not feel that they had a choice.

Second, because it secured their power with the white family.

Third, the maids wanted a mixed colored child, because black women felt the light skin child distracted from their own self hatred of their own racial heritage, and raised their status among black American people.

Even Today, many black women seek to have a light skin baby father by white men ,or Hispanic men, or light skin black men, for the same reasons as our foremothers of old did.

Carrie said, "Oh! And what is that?!

Niqqie exclaimed;

"To distract from their own racial self loathing, hatred of their own black skin coloring. You know historical records indicate that white slave owners brainwashed their black slaves to believe that their black skin meant that they were less than them as humans and cursed.

That is how white people justified in their consciences, to own and mistreat their fellow humans that they kept as slaves:

Niqqie then said to Carrie:
 "Why are you playing stupid? Carrie?"
You know the idea of black people being less than white people was brainwashed into the Psyche of black slaves, by white people".

Carrie replied:
"I am not playing stupid, Niqqie! You have to understand that that I am not having a conversation with you. You are telling me about the circumstances that made you who you are! I am sorry if I sound patronizing to you. I can see that there is so much for me to consider before I can help you. Please continue!"

Niqqie replied, "Okay".
"My grandmother's white family allowed a black Midwife to come in and birth my mother in my grandmother's little house in the back. They named my mother, Ruth Ann Nazareth. They took the last name of my mother's American Indian heritage, because they wanted to protect the sexual action of Mr. Shane Benedict Cavanaugh, the white

owner of the big house".

Niqqie continued:

"As you can see by looking at my skin coloring, that Ruth Ann, my mother has a lot of white blood in her".

My mother, Ruth Ann, considers herself Black American, as does all of the white American society, although she looks white.

My mother has some Creole blood. Her grandfather was French on her father's side and American Indian, or Spanish on her grandmother side. That makes up my Creole blood.

"My racial mix, I am told, is like this.
On my grandmother's side, my great grandfather was English and
My great grandmother was Black.

Nazareth was the last name of Ruth Ann's mother, Lucy Ann Nazareth.

Nazareth was the name of the American Indian who fathered my great grandmother.
My grandmother's last name, Nazareth, is Lucy's American Indian family name.
They had the child, who is my mother, take my grandmother's maiden
Family name Nazareth, to protect the white father, Mr. Shane Benedict Cavanaugh.

Ruth Ann conceived me the same way, by a French white man, but took the last name of my grandmother's maiden family name, Nazareth.

My mother, Ruth Ann Nazareth, racial mix is what is known as Mulatto (which means one white parent and one black parent, although her last name is of American Indian descent.

Lucy Ann Nazareth, my grandmother and Ruth Ann's mother, lived and worked in New Orleans. She had been allowed to stay in a little house at the rear of the big house, Just north of the Mississippi river, where the white family lived.

My mother was conceived and raised in the rear house where Lucy her mother, lived and worked as a maid, with her white family.

Ruth Ann my mother, finished high school while living in the little house in the rear of the big house.

I am told that Ruth Ann was treated by the white family like one of their family.

The white family in the big house ignored the fact that their father had been having sexual relations with Lucy Ann my grandmother, the house keeper, all along.

The three children of the white family ignored the fact that Ruth Ann was really their sister, although they acted like Ruth Ann was not one of them.

Ruth Ann Nazareth my mother was respected in the big house by all the white family members. She was also respected in the school she attended along with all the white children. They respected her, mainly because, Ruth Ann was intellectually more advanced than they were. Ruth Ann was considered gifted and began to read by three (3) years of age, even before she entered Kindergarten.

Nonetheless, Ruth Ann continued to be raised by her mother, Lucy Ann alone.
They continued to live in the little house in the rear of the white family's property.
Ruth Ann's mother, Lucy Ann was strict and did not allowed my mother to be in the company of men alone, black or white.

My mother was enrolled in the Black University where she continued to excel academically.

Carrie then asked Niqqie, "But, how did you come to be born?"

CHAPTER 4

MY BIRTH & MY MOTHER'S LOVE AFFAIR WITH A WHITE MAN:

I continued to talk to Carrie my Social Worker.

"One day while walking on campus in front of the College administration building,

my mother Ruth Ann met this very handsome white man. He was getting out of his car

and dropped some papers.

My mother stopped, picked up the papers, and handed them to

Him. His hands were filled with a briefcase and other papers.

He looked at Ruth Ann and asked my mother to help him carry his things into the

building. My mother took some things in and sat them on the desk in the lobby,

then turned to leave.

The white man put his things down and called to her to wait. My mother had walked out

of the front door.

The white man followed her out of the door and took Annie by the arm and

Said, "Where're you going girl"?

Annie explained that she was on her way to the student union.

He moved very close to Ruth Ann in an intimidating way.

"I'm Mr. Tom Joubert; what's your name girl"?

My mother Ruth Ann spoke very softly repeating her name "Ruth Ann".

My mother was now thoroughly afraid and intimidated by the aggressive nature of the white man.

He assumed that my mother would not resist to the extent that she did.
He said to her, "wait right here Ruth Ann, and I'll be right back.

The white man came back and convinced Ruth Ann, to go with him to another part of the campus, because he said that he did not know the way.

Instead, he drove to his motel and parked his car.
He told her to get out and, "come with me".

Ruth Ann had become thoroughly intimidated and afraid to refuse to do what this white man told her to do.

She followed him into the motel room. He closed the door and immediately hugged her, and started to pull at her blouse to un-bottom it. Ruth Ann my mother realized what was coming next.

Suddenly, Ruth Ann grabbed his hand and held it next to her breast so that their hands were moving up and down, because of the accelerated thumping of her heartbeat.

Ruth Ann screamed, "Wait! Wait! Wait!"

Her sudden outburst startled Tom Joubert, but he continued trying to

Push her down on the bed. But, she resisted strongly.

She realized Tom had become very sexually aroused during their tussling, because his

dick was pushing his pants fly out.

She pushed Tom back and stood up straight.

She said very forcefully, "I am not your little slave girl!!

And I am not going to let you rape me".

My mother Ruth Ann was struggling to overcome the fear inside of herself.

And, she started to cry as she stood there next to the bed.

At that point, everything that her mother had told her about men,

especially about white men, suddenly came into reality.

While Ruth Ann stood crying; remembering her mother's struggles to raised her,

her impoverished living condition, the look that both black and white people

gave her when she passed them, due to her almost white skin color, her lack of money,

her lack of updated clothing. All of these things entered her mind and made her cry

ever more profusely.

But, in this moment, my mom came to a sense of clarity.

Ruth Ann decided to use this white man to help her get through college.

Ruth Ann was determined to finish college.

Then, Ruth Ann stopped crying and said to Tom Joubert:

"I am not going to let you exercise your white mentality over me and fuck me like it's your right! Or, like I have always belonged to you.

I want you to know, I am not your stupid and submissive little black girl that you white men are use to fucking! I have never had sex before! But, I know how and why it's done, and my mother has taught me how this game is played!!"

Tom Joubert, my father, realized that my mom, Ruth Ann, was not going to give in that easily.

So, Tom Joubert became apologetic and said:
"I am sorry; I will take you back to the campus now. What did you say your name was?"

She answered, "Ruth Ann Nazareth, and who are you", she asked.

He answered,
"Thomas Joubert. You may call me, Tom.
When I saw you, you are so sexy and beautiful I could not help myself".

Again Tom tried to pull her in close in to kiss her.

Again Ruth Ann said,

"Wait! Wait!! Can we talk a moment? Who are you really?"

He explained that he was an Attorney from New Orleans.

He was married with two children and had come to the campus on business.

My mother Ruth Ann, explained who she was and how she came to be in College.

Again, Tom Joubert tried to pull her close to him.

This time, my mother let him hugged and kissed her as she stuck her tongue down his throat, as she pressed her lower body on him as though it would meld the two together. At the same time, she made circular movements with her hips.

Tom grunted as Ruth Ann pushed him back, pulled her skirt and top off, pulled her bra strap off her shoulders to allow her perfectly rounded breast to pop out, while Tom took off his pants and shorts.

She pulled her panties off to expose the forest (hair) that hid the fruits of her most private area, and then laid back, opened her beautiful light brown well rounded legs and pulled Tom down in between her legs, and guided his penis into her forested valley of pleasure.

When Ruth Ann cried out in pain, Tom should have known that Ruth Ann was a virgin. Ruth Ann knew that she had started to bleed, but the pain was gone.
She began to allow her body to take over. She twisted her body to get on top of him.
Tom grab at her breast squeezing her nipples to suck them.

Ruth Ann made sounds of satisfaction as her body moved up and down vigorously.

Tom arched his hips upward as he cried out in ecstasy in the words, "make me cum! make me cum!" as Ruth Ann moan in equal ecstasy

Ruth Ann gradually stopped her movements and got off of Tom, as the both of them lay spent.

She said to Tom;
"You know that I was a virgin, don't you?"

Tom said,
"What!! Why didn't you tell me that you were a virgin, Ruth Ann!!

"You didn't ask, Mr. Tom",
Ruth Ann said sarcastically,
"I let you make love to me because I wanted you as much as you wanted me.

Now Tom Joubert, where do we go from here, I am only seventeen for your Information"?

Tom said; "Oh my god, Ruth Ann!"
He offered Ruth Ann some money, but Ruth Ann refused to accept any money from him.

She said to Tom,

"I am no longer a virgin. But, I am not going to let you make me into a whore".

My mother Ruth Ann, explained to me that her accepting money for their lovemaking would make her a whore, in her mind.

Afterward, Tom realized he had developed strong feelings for this beautiful colored girl and he wanted to continue to see her.

Tom gave Annie information on how to reach him if she needed him.

Tom sat silently for a moment, and said,

"I want to continue to see you as often as you will let me.
I will try to be on campus at least once every two weeks".

He gave Ruth Ann his card with office numbers and how to contact him. Then tom kissed and hugged Ruth Ann as though he loved her.

"I grew to maturity in that instant of time. I was no longer a virgin and I had to learn what that meant. My virginity was a protection for me. I could always use it to keep from making a decision to give in to men who want to fuck me; My mind quickly began to adjust to using the incident to becoming free to use her own mental abilities to get my college degree".

From that time onward, my father, Tom Joubert kept my mother Ruth Ann, supplied with money and almost anything she wanted.

I was born one year later November 12, 1960 to Tom and Ruth Ann, when my mother became eighteen and was in her second year in college.

CHAPTER 5

MY FATHER'S MARRIAGE IS THREATEN DUE TO HIS RELATIONSHP WITH MY MOM AND WE ARE HOLLYWOOD BOUND

Carrie my Social Worker asked:

"Did Tom's his wife ever finds out about her husband's elicit affairs with your mother Ruth Ann?"

I replied:

My father's wife, who was once a school beauty queen and friends found out about the baby through their connection with the black communities and, or their maids working for prominent white families of New Orleans.

When Margaret (Maggie) Rosenberg Joubert (Tom's wife) and her girlfriends found out that Tom had secretly fathered a black child; she was not surprised, because white men were allowed by their wives to fuck black women to keep their husbands with them.

It seems that if their white husbands became involved with another white woman, it would break up their family. So, having sexual relations with black women was tolerated. But, this time, it seemed different to tom's wife, Margaret.

Margaret became very angry. She had confronted Tom before, because, she suspected he was cheating.

She told Tom that she thought the reason he kept going to the Black University's campus was to: "Fuck one of those sexy black girls".

Now she had proof that what she and her white girlfriends thought, was right.
In previous conversations among Margaret (Tom's wife) and her girlfriends,
the consensus among them was that white women were prettier, but, black women were much more naturally sexy, despite their color and how they looked; But, how they were shaped, attracted white men to the American black women.

Tom's wife, Maggie, as she was called, decided to confront Tom about "his other black family".

He admitted having sexual relations with Ruth Ann and that the baby was his.

Maggie asked Tom point blank, "Do you love her?" Tom evaded answering Maggie because he did love Ruth Ann.

Tom, not answering whether or not he loved Ruth Ann, made Margaret very angry and she began to verbally and physically attacking Tom, cursing, hitting, kicking, and tearing at his clothes and spitting on him, calling him names, and accusing him of having black blood somewhere in his family because of his darker white coloring.

At the same time their two children, Sawyer (12) and Tara (14), looked and listened in on the fight with profound interest. They tried to intervene to stop the fight.

Margaret ran to the kitchen table and got a knife. She began slashing at Tom and cut him on the hand when Tom threw up his hand to offset her blows.

When Tom's hand started to bleed and blood began dropping on the kitchen floor, Sawyer (their young son) became afraid and told them "I'm calling 911".

Tara (older daughter) tried to stop him from calling, but the call had already been accepted by the operator.

It was only when Maggie saw the blood that she (Tom's wife) realized what she doing. She started crying, hid her face and ran to the bedroom, but she didn't apologize.

The Police and an Ambulance arrived at the same time.
The EMT looked at the cut and said.
"This may require some stitches; get in the Ambulance we are going to take you to emergency".

But Tom said,
"No, This was an accident, stop the bleeding and bandage it up".
The EMTs looked inquiring at the police and at Maggie, who came out of the bedroom and was standing there with them.

The Police said to the EMTs,
 "Do as he tells you!" while looking at Maggie.

After they finished bandaging Tom's hand, they called it in, reporting a domestic accident. The EMTs explained on the radio what they did to stabilize the patient.

After the EMTs left, the Policeman said to Tom and Maggie.

"Let's talk".

The Policeman asked Maggie, "What happened here, ma'am?"

But before Maggie could answer, Tom intervened and said,

"We were playing around in the kitchen and she accidently cut me!

Here is my card. I am an Officer of the court. Do you want me to call the Chief?"

The Police Office knew that meant he could be seen as insubordinate to a court officer, and put in his record.

So, the Police Officer said,

"That will not be necessary Mr. Joubert. I will report this as a domestic accident, instead of a domestic dispute".

Due to Tom's legal influence the Policeman agreed to stop the investigation there.

This fight between, Tom, my white father, and Margaret, forced Tom to use his influence with the Police.

Thus, my father pretended to end his and Ruth Ann's sexual rendezvous.

Tom hugged and apologized to Maggie. But, things were never the same in his family after that.

Tom called his law partner and secretly told his friend and Colleague, Travis Compierte, to draw up papers that would secretly provide for me, his child, and, Ruth Ann, my mother.

So, Tom Joubert continued to help my mother, Ruth Ann, and spent time with her whenever he could.

Tom realized that he love Ruth Ann and would never knowingly abandon her and me, Monique Ann Nazareth (Niqqie) their baby girl.

Tom helped Ruth Ann my mother, to finish her last year in college, enabling Ruth Ann to become a Schoolteacher in Louisiana.

Ruth Ann, my mother, became a part of the elite black fraternities of the black University.

My mother continued to maintain contact with her beloved Tom Joubert in secret.

My mother raised me and kept a close eye on my every move.

As I grew older, I began to rebel against my mother's tight grip on me and monitored my one and every move, so she thought. But, you know, young people will find a way to rebel. I finished high school in New Orleans and started college at the same Black University my mother graduated from in Baton Rouge Louisiana.

Unfortunately, I got involved with the wrong group and got pregnant in my first year of college, but had a miscarriage.

My mother Ruth Ann felt shamed, although she had given birth to me the same way her mother gave birth to her, by having sex with a white man.

Nonetheless, my mother Ruth Ann did not want to face the disgrace she felt among her peers.

So, my mother and I decided to move to Los Angeles California and **we were Hollywood bound.**
We moved to Los Angeles after my first year of college in Louisiana.

When we arrived in Los Angeles, my mother, Ruth Ann, applied and received a California Teaching Credential after she had passed all the qualifying classes and tests about a year later.

I did not start college right after we moved to Los Angeles California, although I told my mother, Ruth Ann, that I had applied.

Carrie the Social Worker said to Niqqie:
"Very good. But, what you have told me, does not really inform me why you left your child alone and defenseless.

But, I have to go now. In our next meeting you must say something that justify why you left your child alone"

Carrie told Niqqie that she would make arrangements for her to come and see her son Kashi at the facility.

Carrie, sensing that Niqqie had other problems other than child abuse, made Niqqie promise that she would stay out of trouble.

Niqqie and the social worker ended their recording session.

This ended Niqqie's first interview with Carrie the social worker.

.

CHAPTER 6

THE STRUGGLE TO UNDERSTAND MY HUSBAND, CHARCOAL

Carrie the Social Worker left, and as Niqqie sat alone, she remembered the many nights alone with Kashi, before she was turned on to crack.

She and Kashi would laugh and play together. Suddenly Kashi would say;
"mommy, will Daddy ever come home?"

That kind of question would always end their playtime,
Because Niqqie loved and missed Charcoal so much.

But now, she realizes that both she and Charcoal, her husband, has turned into complete crack-heads and hustlers.

He was fired from his job as a cook in the restaurant, because of being absent so often from his job. She said to herself:

"Now, I on the verge of losing my job".

Niqqie remembered Charcoal blamed his black skin color for his failure in life.

He often spoke about the impoverished condition his family grew up under.

His father and mother drank heavily as a gateway drug, which led Charcoal to start to drink as a child. He started drinking from the wine and beer left around his house.

Charcoal thinks his anxiety stems from his parents conflicts and living conditions in his home. He thought that was why he eventually sought an escape through drug use.

Charcoal experienced brutality in the home at the hands of his mother and father. They would fight verbally and physically and sometimes take it out on him.

His father presented a weaken father image.

At that point, Charcoal experienced ego conflict causing a feeling of disempowerment, and inadequacy, because of his skin coloring and a strong and domineering mother.

Charcoal felt anger or rage at his mother, father and society.

He also had very ambivalent feelings about his father.

Sometimes, he felt pity and anger, love and hate, guilt and understanding for his father.

But Niqqie thought to herself, what are my reasons for my drug use? My mother did not smoke, drink alcohol, or abuse me or use drugs.

Niqqie chuckled at the thought of her husband's name, Charcoal.

Charcoal had gotten that nickname from siblings and family members on his father's side who are very light skin people.

Niqqie had met Charcoal's parents and other sisters once at a birthday party for his sister Charisa, before she and Charcoal decided to get married.

The story goes that when Charcoal was born, they named him Malcolm Jacob.

His father, Thomas Joe Seberg, who was a very light skin man, looked at the baby and his wife, and the nurses, and Charcoal's two older sisters, Clarissa May and Toni Sara.

He said in front of them all, in his drunken and candid way:

"Roberta May, that boy is as black as charcoal".

So they called him Charcoal as a nickname, ever since.

That remark by his father seemed to question whether Charcoal was his child, and implied that the baby was not his.

That thought had a chilling effect on the relationship between Charcoal's father, Thomas and Roberta.

The oldest, Clarissa, came out very light skin like her father.

Toni Sara, she is the next oldest, came out brown skin.

Malcolm Jacob Seberg (known as Charcoal) came out really dark skin.

Magan Jessica, 4th and last child born to the family, came out dark skin, but not as black as Charcoal.

Charcoal as a newborn baby, although dark skinned, did not have dominant Negroid features.

He did not have a flat nose or oversized thick lips. Charcoal's baby hair was black and curly, like his father's hair. But Charcoal's skin coloring was dark.

Charcoal was the only boy as the third member born in the family of four children, and was the darkest one in the family.

Charcoal's father, already a drinking man, began to drink heavier after that. He began to treat Charcoal's mother more abusively.

In many cases, Roberta triggered such abusive actions from by her husband, because of her, "smart mouth".

She would constantly belittle Thomas and would act independent of his wishes, no matter what they were.

Roberta used her seeming intellectual superiority over Thomas to put him down, or to get the upper hand in family matters of importance.

Charcoal's family gradually grew more dysfunctional.

There appeared to be some color discrimination against darker skin black people by Charcoal's family on his father's side who were all light skin people.

Consequently, Charcoal always had a hard time dealing with his own skin coloring.

Although, Niqqie sensed that on Charcoal's father's side of the family,
who are very light skin black people, shunned Charcoal's mother's side of the family
because of their dark skin.

It seem that Charcoal's sister who was not as dark skin as Charcoal, seem
to be better adjusted to her skin coloring than her brother, Charcoal.

Charcoal's parents finally separated mainly due to his father's heavy drinking and brutality.

Although, he continued living with his mother, she was unable to control him.

After that, the school could not control him. So He was in and out of group homes until he was eighteen.

In Middle School Charcoal was drawn into gang activities (Bloods) after he was protected in physical gang fights by his cousins while in middle school.

After that, he and all his cousins committed themselves to being of the "Bloods", which is a gang orientation.

After numerous arrests as a juvenile, Charcoal was sent to a juvenile camp around age fourteen soon after his father left.

It was there that he got his G.E.D. through the County Juvenile system.

At the same time, as Niqqie was daydreaming, Niqqie acknowledges to herself that the crack cocaine they were now using was in complete control of Charcoal's mind.

Charcoal had stolen or taken many things of value out of their house,
And out of his relatives and friend's homes.

A lot of people were threatening to hurt him when they caught him.

He stayed gone for long periods of time, but would show up
In time for the welfare check.

(Niqqie thought to herself) "In order to keep the apartment, I had to apply for Aid to Families with dependent Children (AFDC), under the working mother's program in order to be eligible, and I had to lie about whether Charcoal was living in the home".

Niqqie reasoned,
"He's gone most all the time anyway. It's like I don't have a husband anyway".

CHAPTER 7

HOW I FELL IN LOVE WITH CHARCOAL

I was at a dance when I first met Charcoal in 1996.

I thought he was quite intelligent despite his only

Recently earning a G.E.D. (high school diploma) while in Juvenile hall.

I thought Charcoal was exciting to be with, and he knew all the latest dances.

Charcoal had just won the Hip Hop dance contest over this white boy Christopher (who was a black boy wannabe). Charcoal and Christopher had met when they were in Juvenile hall together and became friends.

One of my girlfriends that I was with, who was a beautiful dark skin black girl,

She introduced me to Charcoal.

After that hip hop dance contest, me and Charcoal continue to see each other at the mall and different places and at Hip Hop dance concerts.

He asked for my phone number and I gave it to him.

One day I got a call from Charcoal asking me to go with him to a function.

I asked him, "what kind of function"?

He said, "A funeral".

I refused, but asked, "Why would you ask me to go with you to a funeral? that's weird!"

Charcoal explained that one of his cousins, who was just seventeen, had been killed in a gang confrontation in the neighborhood and was being laid to rest.

Charcoal explained that he had never been to a funeral either.

But one of the O.Gs. (Old Gangster) of the Bloods told him to be there.

I told him that going to a funeral was not my thing.
But, it sparked my interest and my excitement about the unknown.

So, I asked, "What do I have to do?"

Charcoal said, "Nothing, just ware something red".

I wore a flaming red silk blouse over a white tight fitting skirt,
With red and white pumps.

So, I picked him up in the car that I had rented and went to the funeral.

To my surprise, it was a respectful, regular funeral (what do I know) but
everyone knew the Bloods were in charge by their wearing red colors.

The dead boy was eulogized and made out to be a nice boy who was in the wrong
place at the wrong time and that is the reason he was killed.

However, Charcoal had told me that the dead boy was one of the main links
to pushing drugs and other gang activities in that hood.

To my delight, I was the most exciting thing at the funeral,

And got more than my share of attention.

After that, me and Charcoal did most social things together.

I gradually began to fall in love with Charcoal, although I knew

that he smoked marijuana and drink alcohol, and was in the gang.

Later, there were two deaths reported in the news in that hood.

One death was due to what the Police said, was retaliation torture.

The man's penis was cut and the face was mutilated.

The other death was due to a shotgun shot to the chest, according to the police report

both of these deaths were considered retaliatory gang activity. That is the way it read in

the news report.

I had not talked to Charcoal for about two days, and when I talked to him, I asked him,

"Did you participate in that retaliation reported in the news"?

Charcoal evaded answering my question. I knew that I should not pursue that issue.

After that time, Charcoal and I became closer than ever. He bought me a beautiful gold

necklace, a diamond ring and other Gifts. He said he would do anything I asked him to.

CHAPTER 8

MY MARRIAGE TO CHARCOAL

Charcoal was nineteen, and I was twenty and living with my mom,

When Charcoal and I decided to get married. We were told by some people

We knew, to go to Yuma Arizona for a quick ceremony.

So, I rented a car and drove to Arizona and got married without my mom knowing.

When we got back we rented a motel room and spent some time together. Later, I went

home to tell my mom.

I told my mom I had married Charcoal in Yuma Arizona.

She was furious with me.

She asked me,

"Is that the thanks I get for raising you and taking care of you for all these years? That

you would run off and marry some little black boy behind my back. Are you crazy!?

Is that the same little black boy you have been seeing for the last few months!?

My god! I didn't think you were that serious!

Are you pregnant" She asked?

I said, "No".

My mom was hurt and refused to talk to me the rest of that day.

She felt that I was disloyal to her and disrespectful of her authority.

But, I was caught up in the black hip hop, pop culture movement that started the transition from black rhythm and blues music in the black ghettos of America, to white popular music.

My mom explained her disappointment in me this way:

"I did what I had to do to get through college, back in racist Louisiana, because my mother was not in the position and, didn't have the money, nor the means, to put me through college, in racist Louisiana.

But, I have good job and is fully able to take care of you, and I am trying to put you through College.
But, you won't let me!

You did not have to get married that way. Why didn't you talk to me, before you betrayed me"?

I told her that I knew if I would have told her,
"I knew you would have tried to stop me".

She said,
"You're damn right; I would have tried to stop you!
Think about what you have done Niqqie! She screamed!
You have tied yourself up with a man who does not have a pot to piss in, let alone a job

to make money to take care of you!

"His black skin is going to work against him and you forever!
Don't you know that!

Where are you going to live? You can't stay here with me.
Think about it Niqqie, you are all I've got!

And now I don't have you anymore!

I thought you would have at least, Finish College, and married a dignified educated man with light skin, who may have been able to take care of you.

Now look what you've got! A gangbanging black boy who will have to literally stand behind you, no matter what you do or where you go.
You had better get ready for that, my darling! He will continue to use you until he uses you up!"

At that, my mom broke into cry, and we cried together, because my mom made me feel so bad.

I realized now that she was right.
My love for Charcoal had blinded me to reality, and I immediately felt regret.

But, most of all, I realized that I married Charcoal because I wanted to get out from under my mother's dominance.

I had decided not to go back to college anyway at that time.

My mother and I ended our conversation with an embrace and we cried together.

Charcoal had been calling and wanted me to come to the motel where we were staying.

I told him that I had to stay with my mom, but I would see him the next day.

The next day, my mom was in a better mood.

My mom said;

"Get up! Let's go apartment hunting and I am going to buy you a car,

But you will have to pay the car note. Agreed?"

I said "Okay".

I called Charcoal and told him what my mom had planned for me.

He was happy and said,

"I knew your mom would do that, cause she is rich. Pick me up and I will go with you".

When I suggested to my mom to pick up Charcoal,

She went off again. My mom angrily said,

"God damn it Niqqie! No! Why would I do that! Don't you get it yet, Niqqie!!

Don't you understand that I am not going to lead that nigger man to believe?

that I am going to use my hard earned money to take care of you and him!

I am only doing this to give you a head start in this god forsaken marriage.

Don't you understand nobody is going to rent you an apartment if they think?

that someone like him is going to be living there.

Later on, you are going to see what a mistake you have made in marrying that black

nigger!.

Let's go, if you want me to help you".

I said, "Okay".

We found a nice used Ford car for five thousand dollars.

My mom put two thousand down and I signed a note for two hundred a month for two

years.

We found a clean small one bedroom apartment in a nice, basically white

neighborhood, for four hundred a month.

The white male manager of the apartment house asked my mom who would be living in

the apartment. He asked if we were married and who else would be living with us.

My mom told him, I was her daughter. She lied and told him, we would be living

together.

Later, my mom said to me,

"Now do you understand, and see why I didn't want Charcoal to come with us"

I said, "Not fully mom, explain it to me ".

She said,

"Because I knew if that white man would have seen Charcoal, that white man

 Would not have rented us that apartment".

I said,

"I guess you are right".

The apartment was furnished with a stove and refrigerator and was very clean.

We bought a used bedroom set and new mattress set, a used couch, and had it delivered the next day.

After that, I had Charcoal come to the apartment in the night.

After we moved in and lived there for a month, Charcoal got a

Job working at one of the fast food restaurants, and we started to do alright.

Later, the white manager said to me when he finally saw Charcoal. "You lied to me".

Chapter 9

THE BIRTH OF OUR SON, KASHI

In the next visit by Carrie my Social Worker continued to talk, she asked,

"So when was Kashi born?"

A chill shot through me as I remembered,
and I said to Carrie,

"No one was allowed to called my husband Charcoal without a
Fight, except me.

I recalled he liked me to call him Charcoal when we were making love.

Every time I think of this one night of lovemaking, a dizzy warm
Feeling would engulf me.

I remembered that one night, because it was special to me.

"I Had never made love, or had a man love me with such intensity
Before that night, and never again since; and I've had
my share of men since I was sixteen".

Niqqie thought to herself.

I remembered, it was one of those hot Los Angeles California summer night around 8:30 pm.

Charcoal and I had arrived earlier that evening from work.

I worked as one in a clerical pool of computer clerks who sent from business to business as needed?

Charcoal worked as a cook in a fast food restaurant.

I was walking from the bus stop, which was a little more than a block away from where we lived.

Charcoal drove by in my car and blew the horn at me, but he continued to drive on.

I was still a long block away front the apartment.

When I walked in the door; Charcoal was waiting. He didn't even speak.

He just said,
"Hurry up and cook, I'm hungry".

I confronted Charcoal about not being sensitive to my needs, and remarked,

"You didn't care enough to give me a ride home in my car; You know the car is in my name, and I am paying the note every month.

Besides, you don't even have a license and, you can't get any credit in your name."

We argued for awhile until Charcoal decided to go out without me again.

Charcoal went in the bathroom to take a shower in preparation to go out.

We had been married about three or four months, and Charcoal had began to go out more and more without me. Charcoal continued to drink and smoke weed, although he had sworn he would stop,

Because as he said,

"I don't want to end up like my pops, on disability but still drinks heavily".

I was afraid to question him about where he was going. My bottom lip tightened as I remembered questioning Charcoal once before, and ending up being slapped and left with a busted lip.

I had sworn to myself, that if Charcoal hit me again like that, I would
purge him from her life, because,
"I was not raised that way."

I remembered feeling especially sexual and sensuous all that day.

I was looking in the mirror as I undressed from the clothes I had worn to work.

As I continued to admire myself in the mirror, I noticed my skin coloring for some reason had turned reddish beige; I guess because I had started to ovulate.

My oblong face was crowned with a head full of semi-straight brown hair, a big forehead, a semi-wide mouth, With medium well rounded lips, and a medium pointed nose.

My close cropped curly brown hair, and almond shaped light brown eyes, gave warning of my mysterious sexual prowess that seemed ready to entrap a man.

My shoulders were slightly square, with perfectly rounded arms of normal length.

My naturally plump breast rounded themselves out with an extended nipple that added fullness to the silken night shirt I had put on without a brassiere.

My naturally small waist and shapely legs extended my 112 lb. firm and shapely well formed frame to 5' 5" tall. Any man would know I am mature, and all woman.

I had stripped down to my panties when Charcoal stood in the doorway of the bathroom.

He was still partly wet while beaded droplets of water sparkled against his black body.

The droplets slid down over tightly woven biceps and the two square humps for a chest, his wet sexual organ seem to be begging to be touched.

His silhouette told of the mysterious sexual prowess both male and Female black Americans are known for.

Just looking at him made me breathe heavily. Standing as he was, it was obvious that he was moderately sexually endowed. He looked taller than his muscular 5' 10" frame.

As I was about to take a chance on my life, by asking Charcoal to allow me to go with him, all the lights went out, and the air conditioner stopped.

It was one of those rolling blackout in Los Angeles during the heat of the summer.

I screamed and Charcoal said,

"It's just a damn blackout; everybody's air conditioner is on tonight."

I said to Charcoal;

"For a second I lost you in the dark. Man! You really are, as dark as charcoal, I couldn't see you for awhile." I said jokingly

Charcoal said,

"What did you say"?

And like a Black Panther, he reached out with one hand and pulled me to him.
When I landed against his chest, it was like hitting a soft brick wall.

He wrapped his arms around me and slowly begin to squeeze.
I tried to scream but nothing would come out.

Charcoal said,

"So you think I'm as black as charcoal. Well, this black boy is going to teach you a lesson tonight."

I became very frightened and began to cry.

Instead of hurting me further, Charcoal bent his head slightly downward and kissed me gently on my neck and earlobe.

My fear began to subside as Charcoal continued to kiss me in the dark.

My arms began to snake around his waist and up his shoulders, as I returned his kiss.

As I pressed my body forward, while returning his kiss; His hands loosened and moved downward to my protruding buttocks. He held them tightly while in a standing position.

Charcoal started to screw with his lower body.

My body began to tremble and my knees gave way.

I Started to drop, but his massive arms held me extended off the floor.
He continued to screw, kissing and embracing me until my body began to go limp in his arms.

He laid me on the bed, on my back. His lips began to suck on my nipples and moved down to my belly button and onto my pussy.

My legs opened and I grabbed his head as my pussy began to pulsate.

He moved up and down my pussy with his tongue, until I became orgasmic.

He turned me over, face down.

He got on top of me and tried to penetrate me.

I tried to accommodate his dick, but he was too big and in the wrong position.
I tried to guide his dick into my vaginal track. I moaned in pain, but suddenly his dick
slipped in because my pussy had gotten so we. He began to fuck me, moving up and
down and I moved with him.

My body became consumed with waves of sexual passion that was building up all over
my body. My pussy began to convulse from the intense sexual feeling.
I was sweating from the heat while my vaginal track pulsated around his dick.

Soon, the sun that was once far away seemed to be getting closer, then streaked down
and allowed it's heat to gently touched me.

We became one, in perpetual fluid continual motion until we cummed together.
Our movements gradually stopped and we lay panting like the animals that we are.

Soon, darkness engulfed me.

I awakened later to find the lights were back on. Charcoal was dressed and about to leave.

He bent over, kissed me gently on the lips, and said,

"You can call me Charcoal anytime, when we are making love, I'll be back later".

He walked out of the door.

I did not answer him, but knew then, I would do anything to hold onto him.

By the next morning, I knew I knew I was pregnant.

Nine months later, our son, Kashimba Joe Seberg (Kashi) was born.

I did not have a bad time during my pregnancy. I had very little morning sickness. I worked on my job up to the last month of my pregnancy.

I was in labor for nine hours. Charcoal was there for the last two hours of my labor. Then, while he was standing there, I grunted and pushed for about 2 minutes. Kashi popped out to the cheers of everybody.

Kashimba was 8 pounds and 6 ounces, beautiful light brown skin, with straight black hair, Charcoal just stood there looking dumbfounded.

Charcoal said, "Let me see! Let me see!"

The nurse held kashi up for him to see and handed him the scissors and said,

"Cut the cord!"

Charcoal said,
"Where?"

The nurse pointed to the cord that extended from between my legs to the baby and said,

"Cut here!"

The other nurse took his hand and guided his hand to the cord.

It was only after Charcoal took a long look at the baby, and saw that the baby was brown skin, with semi straight hair, that he let out a loud laugh with a broad grin and swooped down to hug and kiss me and the baby.

I knew why he had reacted the way he did. It was because he was sensitive about his own skin color, and wanted to see if the baby would be as dark as he is.

The baby boy was born November 10th, at 10:30 PM. We agreed to give him an African name, Kashimba and to call him Kashi. That was six years ago.

CHAPTER 10

THE BEGINNING OF MY DRUG ADDICTIVE BEHAVIOR

Carrie the Social Worker said:

"So you admit that you are hooked on crack cocaine. How did that happen Niqqie?"

Niqqie said:

"Yes I do admit that I am hooked on crack cocaine; But let me tell you how that happened.

At the time I started using, I still loved Charcoal very much". It was because of my love for Charcoal that I became hooked on crack.

Niqqie began to feel warm and tingly as she thought of sexual feelings for her husband. But at this time, the thought of the pain and rage she felt, because her son Kashi has been taken away from her, and her body now craving a hit of crack cocaine only adds to her anxiety.

But, not having Kashi my baby with me jolts me back to reality.

She said; "Kashi is almost seven years old now and we have never been apart. Look at me now; I'm nothing without my baby."

Niqqie began to recount all the things she had done to hold onto Charcoal, and became angrier with every count.

"I let Charcoal talk me into using that damn crack cocaine. I've turned my friends and mother against me.

I've begged, stolen and took food out of my baby's mouth for that, son of a bitch.

I've fucked every pusher in Los Angeles, and I let that lesbian bitch suck all over me for Charcoal, my husband, enjoyment.

Now I've lost my baby". (Niqqie began to cry profusely).

Soon her sobbing subsided, but still whimpering mode, Niqqie continued to remember:

"Damn Charcoal. I had never used drugs before he tricked me into smoking that crack cocaine about two years ago when I didn't know what I was doing."

" I was young and stupid"

I was working and trying to make ends meet; while Charcoal
was running around throwing every penny away he could beg,
borrow or steal, on that crack cocaine.

Charcoal had started on Crack Cocaine four years ago, when he was twenty.
Within two years he lost his job. I had to apply for AFDC to pay the rent and he would

take most of that check.

I had to lie to the welfare people and say he was not living with us to be eligible, by saying he was not in the home. My salary was not enough to pay all the bills.

When Charcoal showed up that day, all I wanted was to be with him.

I remember that he had been gone for about a week.

He failed to show up for the welfare check on the first.
But, there he was, on the 14th of the month to wait for the check on the 15th.

It was raining down cats and dogs. He walks in like he had never been gone, as though he was a good husband just coming in from work, demanding his food and some money.

Like a fool, I fixed him the last piece of ground meat I had saved for Kashi's meal.

I also gave him the last five dollars I had saved to buy gas for the car to go to work on Monday.

I had planned to replace the money I gave Charcoal by borrowing some money from old faithful, Melba, until I got my check on the 15th.

I remember it well; Kashi was watching T.V. at Melba's While Charcoal was gulping down the hamburger like he had not eaten for a long while.

There was a knock on the door. I opened the door and stood half way in the door and asked,

"who is it'?

A stern voice shot back.
 "Flyboy, I want to talk to Charcoal".

My heart jumped into my mouth because everyone knew whenever Flyboy appeared on the scene, somebody had been marked for death.
When Charcoal heard the voice; he jumped up.

Flyboy heard the noise, he pushed the door with a force that threw me against the wall.

I quickly recovered and moved around in front of Flyboy and said,
"Flyboy, please don't hurt him."

Flyboy looked at me from the corner of his eye and slowly his head began to turn until his eyes were riveted on me.

Flyboy said in a slow deliberate gruff tone,
"goddamn baby! who are you and where did you come from"?

I was very scared. Charcoal, which I've always respected as a courageous man now looked weak and helpless.

He was so scared, he lost control of his bladder and urine began
to run down his leg onto the floor.

I was dressed in black tight fitting shorts and an equally snug top.
Flyboy's eyes were like a welder's torch, it seemed.

I could feel my clothes being seared from my body, exposing every curve and forbidden
area.

His raping stare was enough to take a girl's virginity away, without touching her;
but I was no virgin.

I must admit, I was scared, but I did get aroused, seeing this tall handsome muscular
black man standing before me.

I immediately activated my sex hormones and allowed my sexual attraction demeanor
to become apparent in my voice and movement.

This was my defense mechanism against men who get rough with me.

Now I had to use it to protect my man.

I use my sexual attraction like a **tractor beam**.

I knew I had Flyboy caught in the power of my **tractor beam**.

His eyes were following my every move, as I move in between he and Charcoal.

I could see and feel the lust for me being transmitted by Flyboy.

He wanted me, and I knew I had him caught in my tractor beam and could control him.

Flyboy's fists were clinched.

As he continued to look at me, his fist unfolded and his face softened.

He finally turned from looking at me and looked back at Charcoal.

He began to laugh at the gap-legged stance Charcoal had taken due to the urine running down his leg.

Flyboy spoke softer now,

"Hey man, you know I'm not going to hurt you, at least, not in front of this pretty lady . I just want to know when you're going to pay me my money. Who is this beautiful lady?"

Charcoal just stood there still trembling.

I said,

"I'm his wife and we have a child that's next door",

as I moved over to the door that was still opened, and ran next door.

I banged on Melba's door. Melba opened the door.

I stuck my head in the door and called,

"Kashi! Kashi! Come on, let's go, Daddy wants to see you".

Kashi came running because he loved his dad.
Melba said, "What's wrong with you?"

I said, "I'll tell you later if I'm still alive."

Melba quipped,
"what! Don't let that man hurt you again Niqqie, call the police on him".
She thought it was Charcoal threatening me again.

Kashi and I ran back to the apartment. The door was still
Open. We stepped inside to find Flyboy sitting on the couch smoking a cigarette, but I
didn't see Charcoal.

Kashi began calling,
"daddy, daddy, where are you?"

There was no answer. I Walked over to the couch, still feeling that my body had control of Flyboy's mind.

I said,

"listen Flyboy, you ought to be ashamed of yourself, coming into my house and scaring everybody to death. What have you done with my husband?"

I made sure my voice tone was loud, but feminine, so that he wouldn't feel challenged.

I know how the feminine voice tone may enrage some black men, and what happens to women when black men feel that their women are getting out of place and challenging them. They want to start hitting on you, and this big black man will kill me.

Flyboy said,

"Cool it baby, he's in the bathroom getting cleaned up. You want him to look nice for the party, don't you?" Flyboy said, while trying to speak properly.

I realized that when I went to get Kashi, he and Charcoal made some sort of a deal.

Kashi heard bathroom, and went running down the hallway and threw open the door.

I heard a loud slap and Kashi screaming.

I ran to the bathroom and found Kashi standing outside the door crying.

I said, "What happened, Kashi?"

He said, "daddy hit me"

Charcoal's angry voice said,

"Why did you let that boy come in here, can't you see I'm busy?"

I smelled that awful burning scent and there he was, cooking crack cocaine.

I said:

"Well, you didn't have to be so mean and hit him. Come on Kashi, daddy will be out in a little while."

I walked Kashi backed to the living room and quieted him down. I gave Kashi a glass of punch, and walked over to Flyboy.

"Why don't you and Charcoal leave and go do whatever it is that you do. I don't want this going on around my baby. Please leave."

Flyboy stood up and moved toward me. He touched my arm.
I moved back quickly.

He said, "O.K. baby, if that's the way you want it.

When will women like you learn? He's no good; the crack has taken his mind. He can't appreciate a woman like you.

He loves me more than he loves you and your kid", Flyboy said in a lecturing tone.

I looked at him with a sideward glance and said,
"What"?

"Don't even think it." Flyboy shot back.

"What I mean is, he loves anybody who keeps him supplied with crack.
Where's your phone?"

I said,
"I don't have a phone; you are going to have to go somewhere else to use a phone."

Flyboy smiled and said,
"I'll be back when I've finished making preparations for the party."

As Flyboy was leaving, Charcoal came running out of the bathroom.
He said:

"Wait a minute Flyboy, where're you going! Ain't you going to stay and talk to Niqqie for awhile"?

Flyboy laughed and said to me,
"you see".

"Don't worry Charcoal, I'll be back. So that's your name; Niqqie. I like that name".

Flyboy walked on out the door.

I turned to see Kashi embracing his father. I spoke straight forwardly.

"When I went to get Kashi, you set me up with Flyboy, didn't you?"
Charcoal said

"Ahh, look baby, I owe Flyboy three hundred and fifty dollars.
He likes you, and I thought we could have a little party so he could get to know you better.

Flyboy said he's going to pay for everything and give me all the stuff I need and cancel my debt. We'll have a few of our friends over, play some cards, and you know, have fun."

I said,
"What friends, I don't have any friends. You've seen to that.
you mean your crack head friends."

Charcoal slapped me hard across the face and said,
"I said, we're going to have a party."

I grabbed Kashi and ran next door to Melba's.

I told Melba everything. She agreed to let me stay with her overnight.

Melba was not as supportive this time as other times.

She seemed to think I should take advantage of this opportunity to get the money I needed, from flyboy.

Melba told me how Flyboy got his name and that he had a lot of money.

She said,
"I heard he was a Paratrooper in Vietnam, and every time he jumped out of the plane, he pretended he was flying. That's how he got the name, Flyboy

He started to push dope, and got the nickname Flyboy while serving in the war in Vietnam, so his friend said.

I heard Flyboy later killed his friend because the friend stole some dope from him.

Flyboy was a natural killer and was discharged from the Military because of that.

Flyboy had been reared by his grandmother and was one of those black men taken off the streets of L.A. and sent to Vietnam back in the 70s.

Flyboy was not addicted to any drugs. If he was addicted to anything, It was to violence.

His addictive scenario was lack of connection with his mother and father since early childhood and was raised by Foster Parents.

In the military, he had many strong disciplinarian figures who modeled good behavior. However, they could control him only up to point.

He learned to kill without emotion while in the war.

His behavioral pattern became one of violence. He had no real parental direction during childhood.

So, Flyboy took from others what he wanted or needed and gave nothing back..

He never would use crack cocaine however. He wouldn't drink too much either, because he did not like being out of control. He like controlling others.

But, he was known to take really good care of the women he likes, Melba said.

Melba was told that he had a big dick and really could satisfy a woman.

Melba then said,
"I wish he would hit on me."

That made me hot all over again, because he did turn me on when I saw his crotch.

Later, Melba gave Kashi and I a peanut butter and jelly sandwich.
Kashi lay on the Melba's couch and went to sleep.
Melba and I continued to watch T.V.

CHAPTER 11

WHY I GAVE IN TO SEX ADDICTION AND CRACK COCAINE

(I continued to talk to Carrie the Social Worker)

"This is how I got hooked on crack cocaine."

Around ten o'clock, Charcoal knocked on the door. I went to the door and just opened it halfway.

Charcoal said, as he reached in and hugged me around the neck.

"I love you Niqqie, I'm sorry. I don't want to hurt you. Come on over and be with me. We have a lot of food. I know you're hungry. Come on, please."

Deep inside of me, I knew I was going to end up fucking Flyboy that night, especially after that last slap by my husband.

I had been aroused sexually by Flyboy and was hot as a just fired pistol, and I was hungry.

I thought to myself, as Charcoal and I kissed, my body craving some loving.

"If it happens, Mr. Flyboy is going to pay through the nose."

I walked in the door of my apartment, and besides almost fainting from the poignant smell of the burning crack, my ego was immediately crushed. Because, nobody noticed me.

Whenever I entered a party, if the music didn't stop, everybody else did.

Everyone at this party was in their own little world composed of drugs and alcohol. There were thirteen people crammed into my apartment.

The women smoked primo which consist of marijuana laced with cocaine or heroin. The men were free basing.

Others popped pills, used acid (LSD), or shot heroin, or use crystal meth. Everybody smoked marijuana.

When I saw two women sitting on the floor kissing and caressing, I said to Charcoal;

"I want these people out of my house! Right now"!

Charcoal tried to calm me down, "Ahh, come on Niqqie, have a piece of chicken."

I screamed; "I don't want any damn chicken! I want you and your crack head friends out of my house!"

Just then, Flyboy came out of my bedroom. This really made me angry.

I burst into my bedroom, crying.

"What the hell are you doing in my bedroom?"

Flyboy very calmly said,

"Lady, you're messing with my business. You had better shut up before I shut you up."

Charcoal meekly said,

"Niqqie didn't mean anything, Flyboy."

I was really angry. I pushed Charcoal out of the way and got in Flyboy's face.

"Well Mr. Flyboy, you're not going to do any business in my

house and certainly not in my bedroom"!

I found myself pushing him and saying,

"I'm a respectable person, a mother with a child, I'm behind on my rent now and

I'm not going to be put out of my apartment behind this bullshit."

By that time I was crying profusely. I moved to the door and slammed my

bedroom door and fell across the bed. I felt like dirt just being around those people.

About ten minutes later, there was a knock on my bedroom door, but I didn't answer.

Flyboy stuck his head in the door and said,

"Niqqie, come out here for a minute."

I walked to the door and said, "What"?

Flyboy said,
 "See, they're all gone."

I said to Flyboy:
"Good, because I wasn't raised that way. Now you and Charcoal can leave too", as I started to straighten up the place.

Charcoal and Flyboy tried to convinced me to have a drink with them.
I was not a drinking person, but I agreed to have some wine with them.

Flyboy pulled from his pocket a wad of money big enough to choke a horse.

He peeled off a twenty dollar bill and told Charcoal to go and get some good wine, and he could keep the change.

Charcoal smiled sheepishly and left.

Flyboy turned and said to me, "how much do you need for your rent?"

When I told him Five hundred Dollars, he said,

"Here's a hundred on it," and leaned over to try and kiss me.

I moved out of his reach and let the hundred dollar bill drop to the floor.

I evaded his grasp and laughed.

I said to him:

"I have never sold myself, and if I do, be assured, I am not about to go that cheap, not with all the money you have in your pocket".

Flyboy reach over with those massive arms and pulled me into him and started to kiss me hard on the mouth.

This time I let him. I flicked my tongue into his mouth, pressed my lower body forward on him so he could feel the heat, and rubbed his chest nipple in a circular motion with my right palm, then I pulled back from him.

"His eyes walled back for a split second while he grunted. His arms went limp.

His dick immediately hardened and pushed his fly out.

I knew he was caught in my sexual tractor beam once again and, I was in control of him.

I said to him,

"Flyboy, I need five hundred dollars, not one hundred dollars, to pay my rent."

He picked up the one hundred dollar bill where it had dropped to the floor and peeled off four one hundred dollar bills.

He said to me,

"here".

I left him standing in the middle of the floor dazed. He didn't know what hit him.

As I returned from hiding the money, Charcoal walked in the door with the wine.

After getting some glasses, Flyboy and I sat on the couch and started drinking. Charcoal went over to the kitchen table and soon I smelled that odor again. Charcoal was cooking cocaine again.

I said to Flyboy,

"I can't take this. I don't want your money; you and Charcoal have got to go".

But I didn't insist on putting them out.

Charcoal started laughing and seemed happy, he said,

"ahh, honey, it's not so bad. Here, come and take a hit" as he handed me the little pipe.

Flyboy chimed in, "yeah, it'll make you feel better than you've ever felt before."

I said to myself. I need this money, and I know what Flyboy wants. I want to see if my husband will let Flyboy have me.

I knew that I needed to be as high as I could get, if I was going to take Flyboy's dick.

Charcoal fixed the little pipe and gave it to me. I smoked it a little bit and stopped.

After a while I said;

"that didn't do anything for me. I'd rather drink wine".

Charcoal said;

"No wait, you didn't do it right"

.

He showed me how to do it.

I took the pipe in my mouth again, and did it like he told me.

Slowly a strange feeling began to invade my mind and body and shortly, WHOOOSH!

I was there! feeling like I've never felt before. Nothing else mattered after that.

Soon Charcoal began kissing and feeling all over me and I was responding to him.

Suddenly, Flyboy grabbed Charcoal my husband, and flung him across the room.
Then Flyboy started to pull at my tight fitting pants and underwear, until they were at
my ankles. I kicked them off. I tried to move away from him, but he held me tightly by

my waist, lifting me off the floor in a standing position with him.

I looked down, and saw Flyboy pull out his long big black dick from his pants.
I grabbed his big black dick and opened my legs while standing, and tried to guide that big black dick into my pussy, because I was ready to fuck and wanted that big dick in me. But, he was too tall and his dick only rub my stomach.

Flyboy pushed me back into a sitting position on the couch while he held my head and began slapping his long black dick across my face.

He said,
"open your mouth, bitch".

I said,
"no! no! I don't want to suck your dick!"

But, he held my head while he stood over me, and with one hand he continued rubbing the head of his dick in between my lips on my teeth.

I mumbled, but I could not help but open my mouth, as he began fucking my mouth, pushing his dick farther and further into my mouth, moaning in delight until I began to gag. He kept moaning in delight as his dick got harder. I could taste his salty lubricating cum in my mouth. I began to suck his big black dick and It got good to me.
I grab my tits and began squeezing my nipples.
Then He pulled that big black dick out of my mouth that was wet with my spit.
Flyboy picked me up by my hips and twisted me around, bending me over the arm of

the couch with my legs hanging down, then dropped his pants and underwear.

He began pushing his big black dick that was wet with my spit into my pussy from behind.

I moaned in ecstasy while I pushed back. I could feel his dick sliding in.

I grabbed my butt cheeks from behind, and twisted to open my pussy to make it easier for his big dick to go into my pussy. I arched my back, and pushed back in a twisting motion to receive him. He had me by the hips and began to fuck me slowly, in and out, in and out.

I began to fucked him back. His fucking motion from behind became faster, while he moaned in delight, and I moved with him.

I felt my pussy opening and closing, sucking his big dick in deeper and deeper. I was taking all he had to give until I could feel his dick all the way in my stomach.

I moaned, and started to cum like a man.

I cried out in ecstasy and called out his name;

"fuck me! Flyboy, fuck me! don't stop! don't stop!"

My legs stiffened and my toes stretched out to touch the floor, while the intense sexual feeling invaded my whole body. Flyboy began, calling my name,

"Niqqie! Niqqie! oooowi! baby! baby!"

I could tell he was beginning to cum with me. I could feel my pussy filling up with his cum. I took all he had to give, and took him where he wanted to go.

He kept fucking me, until the cum began dripping from my pussy onto the floor.

After it was over, I saw Charcoal sitting in the chair, staring back at me, with his dick in his hand where he had jacked off.

Then Flyboy got off my back, turned me over and stuck his dick in my mouth and said , "suck it".

This time, I opened my mouth and started to suck until I sucked all the cum from his dick, trapping his cum in my mouth.

I got up, ran to the bathroom and spit all his cum out of my mouth. I washed my mouth out until my mouth felt clean again.

My husband Charcoal looked on. But it didn't matter, because the husband kind of love had simply disappeared from my mind when I first got high on crack cocaine.

Even though I enjoyed the sex, nothing can substitute for the crack high and I asked for another hit. "Crack cocaine had become my lover".

I realized then that I had been initiated into the under culture of sexual and drug addiction. That meant, my pussy, and everything, and everybody would be used to support my addiction.

Crack cocaine became my god, my husband, my child, my lover.

My husband and I became drug buddies which was closer than husband and wife.

That meant, we cooperated in keeping each other supplied with drugs from that time onward. Love had nothing to do with it.

Everything I did, from that time onward, I mean everything, became a means to getting more crack cocaine, so I could get high again.

That's why I could so easily leave Kashi my son, alone by himself, with no food.
In the back of my mind, I thought about Kashi, but without the devotion,
without the motherly feeling I had before.

I was totally pre-occupied with finding a way to get my ever-loving crack cocaine;
nothing else mattered at all.

I have never been the same since. It took me ten days after first using crack before I
finally stopped fucking whomever, and using crack.

I paid my rent with the money Flyboy gave me, only because Flyboy kept me
supplied with crack. I didn't go back to work for two weeks.

Later, I went looking for Flyboy for some more crack.

The word was, he had been found dead, killed execution style.

It seems he had come up short of some money and couldn't
account for some crack cocaine that belonged to his supplier.

I was on my own from then on.

Soon, I was out of control like Charcoal.

Now, after more than two years, I had to face being put out of my apartment, I may not have a job, my welfare check is in jeopardy, and I don't have my baby, Kashi.

I told Carrie "I might as well be dead", Niqqie thought as she began to cry again, while she fought off the feeling to get high.

****

Carrie my Social Worker ended our counseling session and gave me an appointed to come and see Kashi a week later at the juvenile facility.

When I arrived there a week later, he ran to me and jumped up in my arms.
Kashi looked great. He was laughing and playing with the other boys at the facility.
He said, "did you come to take me home mommy"?

I was not allowed to see Kashi alone at this time.

Carrie my Social Worker, chimed in and said,
"Not at this time Kashi, maybe later".

Kashi and I sat hugging for a while until one of the boys he was playing with called him.
I told Kashi to go on back and be with his friends.

Carrie, my Social Worker said to me,
"I need to talk with you about Kashi and what we are going to do with him.
I called your mother, Ruth Ann, about taking him to live with her. She declined because as she said,
"I am not in a position to take care of a child at this time".

(Niqqie's mother, Ruth Ann, had all but disowned her when Niqqie married Charcoal. But, she, loved Niqqie and the baby very much. She made herself available whenever Niqqie was truly in need.)

Carrie the Social Worker then said,

" Now, how about you Niqqie, when will you be able to take Kashi home with you"?

That question caught Niqqie by surprise. Tears began to well up in her eyes as she dropped her head and reached over to hug Carrie her social worker, as she whimpered.

Niqqie said to Carrie the Social Worker:

"I know in my her heart that crack cocaine has a hold on me, and is not turning loose. Even now I am craving a hit on the pipe.

Carrie said,

"come over here and sit down with me and tell me about what you are thinking and feeling. It may be that we will have to place Kashi in a Foster home or Group home until you are ready to take Kashi home with you.

We will let some time past, and then we will see" (They went into the conference room for privacy and sat down)

Carrie said,

"Okay Niqqie, what do you think? Tell me about what you are feeling".

Niqqie said,

"I want to be as honest with you as I am with myself, Carrie. So, I will have to start with the last crisis I went through with my bout with drugs to make sure you understand.

It is becoming increasing clear that I am having a hard time controlling my craving for crack cocaine.

Even at this time while we are sitting here with you. I feel I am almost operating out of control. I hope you can help me.

I'll start with the craving for crack cocaine that put me in danger and forced me to seek the drug in very dangerous places and why I had to have an abortion.

As Niqqie tried to remember where to start, she remembered when she got pregnant with a second child.

She told Carrie the Social worker:

I had a pregnancy episode started I had been coerced to go to this crack house with my female crack buddy, Nicole.

It was about one a.m. and she was promised she would be able to get all the crack she wanted for nothing.

I doubted we would get the crack for nothing, and not have to give up anything.

No way. But, she and I knew we had to go. I never liked having her body abused, but, I thought;

"My body is money in the bank."

(Niqqie now knew, she would do almost anything for her new first love, crack cocaine.)

She continued:
"I contacted Charcoal, but found out that, he and his friend Teeki, knew about it already.

The guy who owned the house was a white man who was a cokehead himself.

His name is Christopher, known as Chris, and his wife Tripolie, Known as Trip. He and his wife together were the main supplier of drugs in our hood.

He and his wife were said to head up the gang who was the main contact for the group out Mexico. They were the main contact from Mexico that supplied all the drugs distributed in our hood. They were dangerous people.

I am told that he is also be bi-sexual, and, it was their house where the party, was to be held. I had never been there. They employed a number of homosexuals.

Charcoal my husband had become one of his boys. I decided then, **that I was not going to let Charcoal touch me again**".

CHAPTER 12

CHARCOAL'S HOMOSEXUAL ENCOUNTER

Carrie the Social Worker asked:

"But, why would you not let your husband make love to you again":

I said to Carrie:

"That's another story, are you sure you want to hear about that".

Carrie said,

"If you think it will help me understand you, I want to hear the story. Proceed."

I said:

"Okay, here goes.

Charcoal told me right after we got married, that when he was 8 years old, he and an older boy of 14 was playing around in the apartment when nobody else was home. He slept on the couch in the living room. The older boy threw him down on the floor and started to simulate fucking him. He started to cry and begged the boy to stop. He and the older boy struggled while the boy tried to pulled his pants down and with one hand slapped him across the face and said:

"Shut up!"

The older boy stuck his dick in Charcoal's mouth and said;

"You better suck my dick or I'm going to beat your ass"!

Charcoal said he became scared of the boy and started to suck his dick.

Then, he told Charcoal to turn over and pull his pants down.

Charcoal said:

"I was afraid of boy, so he turned over and pulled his pants down. The boy's dick was really hard. Then the boy told him to get on his knees and bend over. The boy open his butt cheeks and tried to pushed his dick in my asshole until I screamed in pain for him to stop, but he wouldn't stop. Soon the pain disappeared and he kept fucking me in my asshole until he cummed"

Charcoal said that even after he cleaned himself off, he was not able to overcome the feeling he experienced when the older boy fucked him in the asshole.

Charcoal said he let the older continue to fuck him for about a year, until the older boy moved away.

I asked Charcoal was he continuing to have sex with men.
He said no.

I asked Charcoal why did he let the boy continue to fuck him

Charcoal said;

"I was only 8 or 9 years old and I was afraid of the older boy, and besides it got good to me. It was not that I preferred men to women, but I was turned on by the feelings I associated with being fucked in my asshole".

He said the feelings stopped immediately after the boy moved away.

He began to have feeling for females and had his first sexual encounter with a girl when he was thirteen years old. He had told the girl that he had never had sex before.

The young girl, was Fifteen and he was Thirteen. She started to play with his dick until it got hard. The young girl who was not a virgin, guided his dick into her pussy.

Charcoal said he took over from there because he like the feeling he got from having his dick in her pussy and h having sex with a female.

He said the feeling he derive from fucking this girl replaced the feelings he said was in his mind from letting the older boy fuck him in his asshole, and he had not had sex with a male since he was ten years old.

Charcoal was Twenty years old when we had that conversation right after we got married.

When I saw that he had begun to associate with men who are known to be homosexual, I believed he had returned to his homosexual behavior.

In that case, I did not want to expose my health to the HIV virus even though I still love Charcoal.

Carrie Said:

"Do you believe that just being homosexual exposes the men to the HIV virus"?

I said:

"No, but all the ones, both men and women, who are reported to having HIV AIDS that I know off, can be traced back to a man, or have gotten it directly from a man. If I thought that he thought he was infected with the HIV virus, I would not have sex with him".

"Does that answer your question Carrie?"

Carrie answered: "Yes it does".

****

"Now Carrie, can I finish telling you about what happened that cause me to have an abortion".

Carrie said, "go on".

So, I took Kashi over to Melba's place.

When my girlfriend and I arrived at the house, there were some crack heads milling around in the living room. This is what led up to the beginning of my spiraling out of control.

My girlfriend Nicole sent word to me that someone of our group had come into some money and was determined to buy all the crack in L.A. He was inviting everybody he knew.

So, I asked them, "where is the stuff?" Some didn't answer, but another of our crack buddies pointed toward the kitchen.

I walked into the kitchen and who was sitting at the table was this guy we called Maniac, because he was a maniac.

He was suppose to be the main enforcer that worked for Christopher or "Chris", as he liked to call.

I am told that Maniac had killed more people than Flyboy, rest his soul, and most were women.

Maniac had been after me for a long time, because he said,

"I have never fucked a woman as fined as you".

but I had stayed out of his grasp. I had to run from him twice before.

He is a gang member who worked for this supplier and his business is killing people.

Everybody was afraid of him.

My girlfriend immediately grabbed my arm and started to pull back when she saw him.

But it was too late. He had already seen us.

He had his right hand on one of the biggest pistols I had ever seen in my life.

He picked up the gun and pointed it at us and said:

"Hey! don't you run! come over here!"

My girlfriend started to tremble and her short nails were cutting into my skin.

My street motto and advice to women are:

"Whenever a man gets angry and want to turn violent with you, don't get mad, get sad, because to struggle with them will only make them feel challenged".

.

I get real feminine with them, hugging and stroking them, hanging onto them for dear life. Because, most times a female addict's life is in danger all the time, and may depend on getting him to control his anger, under these kinds of circumstances.

Most times I get away without getting slap around or beat up, or giving up my precious body. It didn't work this time, however.

He had me at his mercy because I needed that crack.

I gripped my girlfriend's hand and walked over and stood along the side of Maniac, and pressed the left side of my body onto his right arm holding the gun, so my **tractor beam of sexual heat** could bring him into control.

My left hand slid around to his neck and left shoulder and up his neck onto his face, softly pinching his left cheek.

I could see and feel that my, sexual tractor beam had him and he was under my control. He looked up at me, weakened by the tractor beam of my sexual heat.
His mood immediately change and he put the gun down and his face softened.

I said as softly, and as feminine as I possibly could,
"what do you want baby"?

He said, "I just want to talk to you Niqqie, but you keep running away from me."

I bent my head down close to his ear and said in a whisper while kissing his earlobe,

"here I am baby, talk to me."

He grunted, and suddenly his left hand shot under my skirt in between my legs, like a ripsaw, grabbing at my pussy as we felled back.

My girlfriend screamed. But His move didn't panic me, because I was used to men making sudden and unexpected moves on me.

I grabbed his arm with my thighs, held his hand in place so he could feel the heat of my pussy.

He thought he had me, but I had him, wrapping my arms around him, with my face pressed to his face, holding on, with my lips still sucking his earlobe.

He cried out, "ooowie Niqqie"!

I said softly,

"Crack may put me on my back, but how much money do you have."

He said,

"I have a $100 dollars in my pocket, take it"

I reached in his pocket and pulled out the money. He had 120 dollars. I put 20 dollars back in his pocket and kissed him hard on the lips.

He jumped up, his arm ripping my skirt. He picked me up and started to carry me out, leaving the gun and the box with all the stuff on the table.

I knew if he would have left that box with all the drugs in it, and it would have been taken; he would have killed everybody in the place, and I would not have gotten anything for what I was going to have to go through.

So, I said to him,

"get the box of drugs, get the box of drugs"!

He turned and put the gun in the box, and picked up the whole box

of drugs that included heroin for the speed ball, while still holding onto me and carried

me and the drugs into a side room.

I thought we were going to get high together first.

I found out he was already high, and was only interested in my body.

He put me down on the floor and that maniac started tearing at my clothes.

I said,

"Wait a minute"!

I finally got him to settle down. I intended to make this ordeal as short as possible, by

bringing him as close to ejaculation as I could before I gave in to him.

I let the money dropped to the floor, unbutton my blouse and took off my skirt, leaving

my panties and bra on. I slowly dropped the bra strap off the left shoulder allowing my

left breast to pop out to tantalize him. I asked him to allow me to smoke a primo.

But, before I could get the words out of my mouth, he was on me. He tore off my

panties and plunged himself between my legs. I knew I had to end this, before the

maniac killed me.

So, when he plunged forward, I raised and open my legs, bent my legs at the knee, cupped my arms under his shoulders, twist my pussy to allow his hard dick to enter my cock. I could not help but cry out,

"ooowe! push it! push it in!"

I arched upward allowing his penis to enter my vaginal tract, suspending his lowered body in midair for about a minute, while my hips screwed him, while the right muscles in my pussy milked him. My arms held him tightly.

When I let him down, he started to shake, and jerk, and moaning curse words.

It was over in no more than one minute.

I let him lay between my legs but kept my lower body moving underneath him until I could feel he was getting hard again. It felt good to be under his wide big body and I wanted to fuck now more than ever.

I reached down and felt his dick was getting hard enough to go back in.

I began to fuck him as my wet pussy sucked his big hard dick in.

He raised up on his elbows and began to fuck me again. I fucked him back until my pussy started to convulse and he started cum again. I reached my orgasm and he cummed again, filling my pussy up with his cum.

I rolled him off me as he lay panting.

I picked up the $100 dollars off the floor and put my clothes back on, except my panties, because that maniac tore them off me.

I found a bathroom and cleaned myself off.

I returned and looked at him and said,

"Now, maniac you got what you wanted, what do you have to say for yourself?"

He said, "I love you Niqqie".

I said,

"Okay Maniac, are you going to try and hurt me again?"

He said, "no"!

I said to him,

"remember, you're my baby now",

That brought a smile to his face and he laughed out loud. I saw he was still somewhat

dazed, because I had fucked his brains out, and enjoyed every moment of it.

I asked him for my crack. He told me to take what I wanted from the box.

I took six primos and some rocks and a little meth and left him sitting there on the floor.

I went back into the living room and found a corner with my girlfriend.

We started to get high.

Soon I was the center of attention and everybody started calling for my sex dance.

The sexual moves came natural to me. My girlfriend and I went into motion.

That was when Charcoal and his male homosexual friend came out of their hiding place to see me and my girlfriend dance.

I must have had sex with at least three more men and one woman.

She was all over me trying to screw me without a dick.

While I was high, she got between my legs and put the lips and pearl tongue of her pussy right in my wet pussy. While in between my legs, she moved her little hips in a fucking motion in my wet pussy so that her pussy lips and pearl tongue seem to grip my pearl tongue while she sucked on my tit nipples. I could not help but love her back. I must admit she did make me cum.

I made love to her for the remainder of the time. It was good, but I laugh at her and got out from under her. I pushed her away because I am not a dyke. I slept for almost two days after that two day period.

The next month, I missed my period and I knew I was pregnant.

I went to my friend Melba and told her everything. She asked me who the father was.

I broke down crying and told her I didn't know. I wanted Melba to come down
on me hard, but she was so understanding, it made me sick.

I called her a hypocrite because nobody is that nice and understanding.

Melba got mad then, and said she was not going to help me.
But she finally broke down and told me about an old white woman
she knew who had helped some other women that wanted to get
rid of their babies.

I was afraid to go to my mother to tell her I was pregnant, because I knew she would criticize me severely.

This time, the only way my mother found out about the abortion and that I was in the hospital; was when the hospital called her and told her I was going into surgery.
The hospital was unable to locate my husband, Charcoal.

Chapter 13

THE NEED FOR AN ABORTION

Then Niqqie decided to tell Carrie about how she came to needing an abortion.

Melba suggested that I wait to see if my period would come.
She also thought I should go ahead and have the baby because that would increase my welfare check. I rejected that idea because I hated the welfare system.

I hated the nice-nasty way the workers treated me; especially the black workers.
They were downright cruel to their own people.
They didn't like me because I looked like I was white, but when they found out I wasn't white, I would be treated worse than ever, not that those black women didn't treat every black person bad.

I never thought I would ever come to having an abortion.
But there I was, two months pregnant, not knowing for sure who the father was, and getting ready to have an abortion.

God! here I am, waiting to see some mysterious woman about having an abortion, that I thought at the time most probably has four sets of eyes, three sets of arms and ten legs.

I suddenly became very frightened. I jumped up from the couch where I had been told to sit, and was about to run out of that hellhole, when this tall stately white woman appeared at the door.

As I turned to walk out of the door, I heard an authoritative but soft voice say;

"About to change your mind, huh, I understand. But, let's talk about it first."

I obediently turned around and walked over to her, and fell into her arms, sobbing my eyes out.

She said;
"I can see you are having a hard time, are you in pain"?

I said, "no."

After she had gone through a couple other reasons for tears, with my answer being "no," to all her questions.

She said;
"why are you crying then"?

I looked at her and said:
"Because I'm glad you are not big and black with six eyes, six arms and ten legs."

The white lady got a big kick out of that. Then she said in a condescending way, "what would be wrong with that"?

I ignored that question.

Terry was the lady's name. She was doing her bit for the pro-abortion movement as a nurse practitioner.

We talked for a long while about everything except my drug problems. I felt good because I hadn't had a hit for over a month.

I thought I had it out of my system, so there was nothing to discuss.

Terry gave me the address of the abortion clinic where I could go to have the abortion, after she informed me of the dangers of having an abortion.

I knew I had a serious drug problem and I had been out of control, and I just couldn't have a baby, not knowing which one of those crack heads was the father, "no! No way".
That is why I decide to get an abortion.

So, I accepted an appointment to have the abortion that following Monday.

I had been going to work on time for about ten days straight, and I had not used drugs for a long time.

So, when I went to work the next day, which was Thursday, I put in for five days sick time.

My supervisor called me into her office, I thought to discuss the time off, but it was really to lay me off for excessive tardiness and too many days off.

So, now I was really feeling ashamed, guilty and frightened.

However, I was determined not to use anymore crack cocaine.

I went in and had the abortion.

The doctor placed me on the table, gave me a local and general anesthetic, went in between my legs and did what abortion doctors do.

I asked to see what he had taken out of me.

But, I was sorry I did, because it made me sick to see what I had just done to my second child, who was a girl.

I started crying and had to be consoled, because I kept apologizing and saying to the fetus, "I'm sorry".

I kept bleeding and had to be hospitalized. After that I felt really clean. I had lost a lot of weight, but I felt good otherwise.

That is how I came to needing and having an abortion.

Afterward, I decided to call my old supervisor, Connie, (who was a very light shin mature woman who reminded me of my mom), the day after the

abortion, to see if I could get my job back.

For the first time, I told her about my Crack cocaine addiction and tried to convince her that I was no longer addicted.

We talked about how bad some black men treat their women, and how some men react when their wives demonstrate more smarts than they do.

My supervisor made me see that it was because of my husband that I got hooked on crack cocaine. She pointed out how we black women had to stick together.

The bottom line was, she was going to allow me to return to work. I was to report to work on that next Monday. I felt good about that.

I started to spend some quality time with my son Kashi. I was beginning to feel again.

I even called my mother and took Kashi by to see her.
She acted all mean, but Kashi steals her heart every time.
She even gave me some money to buy Kashi some new clothes.

It was then that she told me about my white father, Tom Joubert the white Frenchman from Louisiana. She said, he had called her and told her that he and his wife Margaret were in the process of getting a divorce.

He told my mother, his old lover, that he loved her and wanted to be with her.
He had been invited to join a law firm here in Los Angeles, and he would only be here for two days. But, if he was accepted into the Law Firm, he may be moving to Los Angeles for good. He said his daughter Sara, was with him and wanted to see her black sister. He asked to come and visit my mother and I.

My mom lied and told him that my job had sent me out of town for the week, but they could come by to see her.

My mom said he came by with his daughter Sara.

My mom said: "Surprisingly, Sara looked a lot like you".

Sara hugged and kissed her and said to my mom,

"I am looking forward to seeing my sister Niqqie. When are you going to let me see her? You know I have never seen her, don't you ".

I asked my mom if she would would consider marrying my father Tom Joubert if he asked her.

She said,

"I do love him, and I believe he loves me, you are proof of that; but I don't want to start thinking of that scenario unless it was here and now. Believe me, If it happens, that would be the next story of our lives that we could write about".

We dropped the subject.

On Saturday morning, who would come knocking at my door but, Charcoal.

I believe that man can smell when I have some money.

Of course, you would know he wanted some money.

There he was, looking sick and pitiful.

My love for him started to re-emerge again. But I knew if he stayed around, I would end up using crack cocaine again. So, I gave him twenty dollars, and told him to leave, but he saw I had a hundred dollar bill my mother had given me, in my purse.

The next day, which was Sunday, Kashi and I went to church.

I was beginning to feel like my old self again, when Melba came over and told me Charcoal was on the phone and wanted to talk to me.

I started not to answer the phone, but I talked to him.
He said he needed a place to crash for one night.

I finally agreed to let him stay for one night. I told him I was not going to have sex with him, he would have to sleep on the couch. I question him about whether or not he was he was having sex with the known homosexual that I saw him with. He said,
"Oh he is just a friend".

I cannot say that in the back of my mind, I didn't know what was going to happen that night.

The thought of being with Charcoal my husband, an old drug buddy, made me feel that desire for crack cocaine again.
It came surging through my mind again. I continually tried to convince myself I was not going to give in to Charcoal, or my feelings to use crack again.

I know I didn't want to have sex with him because he had been messing with that homosexual that looked sick.

Charcoal came in about 9:00 p.m. We sat on the couch and talked for awhile. I could smell the cocaine on his body. He saw that I was getting anxious.

My head seemed to be filling up and all my thoughts began to race through my mind in one line saying,

"get high, get high, that's the only way you can stop the pain."

Charcoal chimed in and said,

"here, I brought you a hit."

When I saw the rock of crack cocaine the racing in my head stopped, as I looked at the two rocks in his hand.

I became extremely angry at Charcoal at that point. I believe I could have committed murder that night. I called him everything but a child of God, because he knew what he was doing to me. He had set me up to fall, just like he did the first time.

Charcoal kept saying he was sorry, but he couldn't help himself.
Finally I stopped crying and took the rocks and a marijuana joint and prepared to get high once again.

Soon, my tears turned to laughter, and I ruled the world once again. Charcoal begin to touch me and arouse my feelings for him once again.

Although I had sworn I would never have sex with him again. It seemed my whole body became one bundle of sexual sensation.

Charcoal started to hug and kiss on me and the old feeling returned with a fury.
I had dressed for bed and had on my new silk pajamas. I unbutton my blouse and he started sucking on my nipples.

He knew that always make me want to fuck.

Charcoal pushed me back on the couch and I pulled my pajamas off and opened my legs. Charcoal moved from sucking my tits to sucking my pussy.

He acted as if he wanted to eat me alive.
I grabbed his head and began moving it from one sensitive area to the next.

I cried out, "suck it! ooowi baby! suck it!" as my pussy fucked his mouth until I became orgasmic and lay spent breathing hard.

He moved to put his dick in me but I closed my legs and would not let him in.

He got angry and began cursing me:
"Goddamn you Niqqie, open your legs bitch" and he slapped me hard across the face.

I said, " No! no! get the fuck off me! I don't know what you've got! I am going to call the police!"

That's when he said, "okay, I don't want you anyway! it's not worth it!"

Nonetheless, I knew that the cycle of addiction had picked up for me again where it left off.

My husband, old drug buddy asked me for some money to go out and get more crack. I gave him my last 30 dollars.

Now here I am again; faced with chasing after our ever loving crack again with husband, who is my drug buddy.

But, I was determined to, not let my ever loving crack lead me down that road again. I knew that I had a fight on my hands.

I knew that I had to develop a plan to resist my longing for the drug. I knew that I had to get away from being around anything, and anybody that reminded me of the high I felt from crack cocaine.

The anxiety level began to engulf me and build up in my mind again and my body was feeling tense and nervous.

Fortunately, my baby Kashi was safe as he could be in a foster home.

The next day I went to Melba who had my social Worker's number to call and asked Carrie my Social Worker to see if I could have the phone number to the facility to talk to

Kashi my baby. I asked Carrie if I could go by to see kashi.

Carrie said,

"no, you do not have visitation rights at this time without me. Later on, I will pick you up, and take you to see Kashi".

Carrie said that she wanted me to go and join an Alcoholic Anonymous group in the meantime.

I called my mom and asked her to go with me. My mom surprisingly agreed to go with me.

CHAPTER 14

THE AA MEETING, REVEALING OF SEX ADDITION NYMPHOMANIA

So, I contacted an old friend, Corrina Bea Scott and asked her to introduce me to the counseling group she was attending.

When we arrived at the meeting place, we were greeted with skepticism. By that I mean, most of the 10 people looked my mom and I up and down without saying a word, which was un-nerving, but I could understand their skepticism.

My mom and I looked alike and was Caucasian looking; very light skin, straight hair, and same height.

There were three of us, my mom, and my girlfriend who was a member of that group of recovering addicts, which made 13 in all at the meeting.

The meeting was handled by a Therapist who was the moderator, who happen to be an Irish white lady, who herself was a recovering addict.

She opened the meeting by saying, "Most of you know me, but for those who do not; My named is Josie Antoinette Maldonado. You may call me Josie, or Ms. Maldonado. It is all the same to me".

We all were mingling around before sitting down trying to get acquainted while engaging in small talk, when a lady with smooth dark features, who happen to be black American, looking to be in her middle forties came in the door. She was of medium height, 5 feet, stocky built, good looking, but African dark. She just stood there starring at me from the side.

The moderator spoke to her by name.

"Chelsia, would you please have seat".

The moderator asked that all visitors have a seat in the side chairs. My mom moved from beside me to the three side chairs at the side of the room.

Chelsia took my mother's place in the chair beside me.

Chelsia said in a low tone to me.
"I can't wait to hear what you have to say, miss lady".

The moderator Josie spoke up;
"Corrina, you have brought with you today someone whom you have indicated would like to join our group, if that is so, would you please stand and introduce her to us".

Corrina stood up and said,
"This is my friend, Monique Nazareth, known as Niqqie, and that is her mother, Ruth Ann Nazareth, sitting in one of the side chairs. Niqqie would you please stand and introduce yourself to the group, and tell us why you are here".

Niqqie stood up and said;

"I am Monique Ann Nazareth. I am known as Niqqie. My mother, Ruth Ann Nazareth came with me today to show her support for my decision to seek help to control my addiction, so that I am no longer out of control. I am at the point where I must admit that I am an addict"

At this point, Josie the moderator said,

"We would like to welcome you to our group, Niqqie".

She continued:

"The mere fact that you have come to us voluntarily indicates that you are willing to allow your motivation to use drugs to be examine, and you are willing to accept criticism without anger and retaliation. Do you agree to what I have just stated Niqqie?"

Niqqie answers; "Yes".

The moderator then said;

"Mavis, as the Secretary, please make the motion":

Mavis stood up and said,

"I move that we accept Niqqie as a member of our group without prejudice. Do I hear a second to my motion?"

Corrina, who brought Niqqie to the group said,

"I second your motion"

Mavis said: "It has been moved and seconded that we accept Niqqie as a member of our group. All in favor, please say, I agree"

All said, "I agree".

Chelsea, who had sat down beside me, but kept mumbling to me,
"why don't you go somewhere else".

I just looked at Chelsia, but I could feel the tension mounting in the room.

The other members started to laugh.

Josie the moderator said;
"Mavis you will see that our new member get a copy of our charter to sign, won't you?"

Then said:
"Chelsea, don't start with your angry rhetoric. I want this to be a session that is informative and beneficial to all of us and a reason to maintain our sobriety. If we allow anger, and jealousy, and envy to take over our being, we will be back on the drug in short order. Don't you agree Mavis?".

Mavis was a tall male who looked to be of American Indian descent, but with some black features. He was the secretary of the group and was a controlling figure.

He spoke right up and said,
"Chelsea would please shut up so we can get this session underway".

Chelsea shot back;

"you shut up Mavis, because you still haven't explained how you got that red skin. Is

that why you became a dope head, ha! ha!?

Mavis responded,

"I guess you got your black skin because you were born and raised in a coal mine and

couldn't get the black stuff off, ha! ha!!"

The moderator step in and said, "stop it you two!"
At that, the group quieted down.

Ms. Josie Maldonado the moderator said,

"Since we on the topic of ethnicity, let's continue that topic. I want each of you to think

about what role your race or ethnicity played n your becoming a drug addict, if any.

Can we all agree to that kind of discussion?"

Chelsea said:

"yeah, let's start with the two white bitches, what did you say your name is"? while

Looking at me.

Ruth Ann, my mom said, "who are you calling a bitch"?

Chelsea said, "if the shoe fits! wear it!"

Before I could say anything, the moderator interrupted.

"Let's get one thing straight, Chesia. I am in charge of this meeting and I am going to ask you one more time to allow this meeting to be orderly. If you can't do that Chelsia, I must ask you to please leave! Do I make myself clear, Chelsia? You along with all of us, agreed and signed the Charter to be respectful of each other's right to speak.

Do you still agree with that statement in our Charter, Chelsia? Please answer, yes or no"?

Chelsia answered, "yes".

The moderator Said; "Mavis, please give Niqqie a copy of the charter to sign"

"Good, I'll begin this part of our meeting by confronting my own ethnicity and telling you about my own addiction and how I became addicted. Just so you know that I am a kindred spirit, I too, am a recovering addict from alcohol and another addiction that I want you to identify.

You may stop me to ask questions to clarify what I am relating to you. After my lecture, I'll take questions.

Ms. Josie Maldonado continued;
"Although I was born in the United States, my parents were not. They are of Irish descent born in Ireland. That would make me a white female of Irish descent, which is an ethnic group.

My parents migrated to the United States before I was born, after they got caught up in the Political / Religious conflict in Ireland; Protestants against Catholics. I had two brothers that were born in Ireland before my mother and father migrated to America. My older brother stayed in Ireland and continued to be a part of that conflict in Ireland. He was later killed as a part of the Protestant movement.

My mother was born in a Protestant family in Ireland, and my father in was born in a Catholic family there. I was born 6 months after my parents arrived in the United States

In Ireland, there was constant bickering between my mother and father and the two families; each one demanding that my brothers and take the side of one, or the other.

We did not know what to believe. So, my brothers and I would try to block out their arguing the best we could.

We did not know which side was right, and didn't care. My father and my mother were heavy drinkers and we were allowed to drink in the home. By the time I was in the 12th grade, I realized I was addicted to alcohol, and I dropped out of high school.

One member asked, "Did you enter a program then"?

Josie answered;
"No, my parents ignored, and or, didn't understand the seriousness of my problem. So I was allowed to try and handle my problem by myself. They continued to keep alcohol anywhere in the house, because the culture of my people allowed ultimate freedom to use alcohol to treat all emotional problems. My culture did not allow for the restriction of

alcohol to anyone.

In America, my parents continued to emphasize the importance of education, despite being fully aware that I was drinking heavily.

But, I knew that drinking alcohol had impeded my study habits to the extent I could not study effectively. I was failing, so I dropped out.

After a time I managed to stop drinking. I went back to school the next year and got my diploma. I got a job and moved out of my parent's home. I thought I could control my drinking if I was not around all that bickering.

After high school, I entered college and changed my work hours to part time. I realized that I could not function while going to college and working at the same time. But, I fought off my craving for a drink and was doing very well. I stopped drinking for about two months.

CHAPTER 15

SEX ADDICTION (NYMPHOMANIA) REVEALED

The Moderator Josie continued:

Then, I begin to fall behind in my rent and other bills. I began to have a drink or two once again. Soon, I was out of control and drinking constantly. Soon, I was broke and wondering how I was going to pay my rent.

My girlfriend, whom I knew always kept money, said she was not going to loan me anymore money, but she would show me how to earn some money.

She introduced me to another female friend of ours named Charlotte, who had the sex connection. Charlotte said she would put me on her list. She took sexy pictures of me. Soon I was receiving phone calls from men asking me for dates.

My first date asked me to be one of a threesome for fifteen hundred dollars, two men and me. I knew I had to get drunk in order to do that but I did not want to start drinking heavy again, but I needed that money bad.

They offered to send a car for me, but I refused, because I wanted to be free to leave whenever I wanted to leave.

So I got the address of the Hotel and took a cab there. They paid me one thousand five hundred dollars up front. I had agreed to deliver Five hundred to our friend with the connection and one thousand I kept for myself.

This sexcapade went on for about three hours until the men couldn't take anymore.

Yes! I fucked their brains out and loved every minute of it.

After All the alcohol was gone, and I was near to passing out, I had them call a car to take me home. That thousand dollars allowed me to catch up my bills.

The next morning I had a terrible hangover, but wanted another drink.

Beside, my desire to continue drinking, I became overwhelmed for sexual intercourse right then. I was like a hereon addict coming down, and needing another fix.

My mind kept recounting the sexual feeling I felt when engaged in the act, creating further desire for sexual intercourse. **That was when I realized that I had another addiction.**

Moderator Maldonado stops at this point and asked the group;

"Who of you can tell me what is going on in my physical and emotional system at this point?"

Miriam said, "Your sex addiction kicked in".

Ms. Maldonado the moderator replied;

"You are correct Miriam. Besides craving alcohol, I am now craving sexual contact. What is the name society gives a women who craves sexual intercourse?"

Miriam again raised her hand and replied, "Nymphomaniac".

"Correct again Miriam.

From then onward, every time I craved a drink, I was looking for a man to fuck me.

How many of you know what Nymphomania is"?

Gladys, another white girl raised her hand.

Ms. Maldonado said;
"all right Gladys, tell us what you know".

Gladys said; I don't know much about nymphomania because I don't have that problem, I would rather have sex with a woman using a dildo....

The moderator interrupted and said,
"Oh! so that means you are not also a nymph?".

Before we go any farther with that topic, let me finish my experience.

After a year of therapy I decided that my sex addiction was tied in with my addiction to alcohol, and the only I was going to get my sex addiction in control was to stop drinking.

So, I stopped drinking again, and went looking for part time work again, because I laid myself off of my last job.. I was referred to another counseling center as a clerk. After I explained my condition to them they decided to hire me. I took the job.

My craving for sexual intercourse gradually subsided as long as I wasn't drinking. I changed my college major to Counseling and went on to get my Masters. I was referred to this agency as a Counselor when I got my Masters, and here I am.

If any of you feel that my experiences can help you. Please feel free to consult with me privately.

Cynthia, one of the group, spoke up and said,
"You were able to get a number of good jobs during your trouble years. Any one of those jobs would be lifetime employment for many black men or women; How were you able to move from job to job so easily, and why is that so?"

(Out of the thirteen people in the room, 9 were considered black Americans. They all clapped)

Josie replied; "I didn't want to get on the subject of race in America; But since you brought it up; Let's go there.

My studies in early American History and Anthropology teaches that America was initially settled by members of the Caucasian race of people (that means white people) from the European Continent, i.e., English, Irish, France, Germany, Sweden, Italy, Spain, Russia; These Countries are what may be called progressive civilized Countries.

What that means is, Countries such as these already had a system of social cooperation that enabled them to be peaceful within and outside their communities. They had developed a system of maintaining their individual family wealth through an inheritance system for individual families already in place before they migrated to America. This idea of family inheritance was instilled in them from birth. So, when they migrated to the American Continent, although under hostile circumstances, they were ahead in socialization, industrial inventions that extended their understanding of how to use their mental powers for the good of their family and their race. This collaboration technique increased their power as a people when they collected themselves as a Nation.

When these mainly European people established themselves on the North American Continent, they sought to collect themselves into individual family structures that was molded into a force that solidified their power of communicating their will over the world population through the use defensive dominating military practices, monetary policies (the forceful movement of money as a means of exchange called capitalization), the use of the power of the Christian Religion as a dominating social force in America.

Over the last 5 hundred years, the building up of each individual family structure enabled the American white race to pass their physical and monetary resources down to individual's families, i.e., the "Rockefellers"; and the Caucasian (white) race as a whole to be used whenever the need arises.

That is why, when any one member of the white Irish family is in need, the white Irish family structure will come to their aid.

This is the kind of family social structure like that in England, France and many Countries in Europe that these immigrants to the American Continent, sort to enlarge upon as a "perfect Union". Can you understand my analogy?

So, when I, as a member of the white Irish American family structure needed help, any one of the white American race, felt obligated to help, as my continued employment demonstrates.

You must agree with me when I say, black Americans have not built up that kind of inherited social family structure with resources, as a race or social structure, that is able to respond to the needs of employment of any one member of the American black race, yet.

I believe it will take another 50 or more years for the American black race to equal the kind of social structure that American white people have developed over the last 500 years.

I hope I have explained in general, why white Americans have higher employment statistics than black Americans. Any further questions?"

Chelsea said, "let's go back to the meaning of Nymphomania"

Ms Maldonado said , "okay, Mavis, take the dictionary from the shelf and look the word up in the dictionary"

Mavis found the word in the dictionary and began to read:

"Nymphomania;. Abnormal and uncontrollable desire by a woman for sexual intercourse".

Gladys said; "See! What did I tell you?"

The Moderator said; "All right Gladys. The word Nymph traditionally refers to a woman. But mania refers to the behavior. If you remove the word Nymph and replace it with sex, making the word , sexomania, could the same meaning be used to describe the sex behavior of a man"?

Salvo, a Hispanic man who looks like a woman, spoke up and said;
"Yes"

Chelsea said to the homosexual; "You're a weird looking bastard".

CHAPTER 16

My MOTHER, RUTH ANN GETS ANGRY

I could not help myself, and the words just came out:

"Chelsea, you can't talk about how anyone looks, because you look like a man yourself."

Chelsea turned to me and said;

"Who are you calling a man, bitch", and slapped me hard across the face that almost knocked me out.

I fell back in the chair and the chair and I tipped over and hit the floor.

My mom Ruth Ann, jumped up out of her seat and grabbed Chelsea from behind. She was on Chelsea back before Chelsea knew it.

My mom was a peaceful woman, but was trained in self defense techniques.
She was in good shape, because she worked out every day.

My mom, Ruth Ann, grabbed Chelsea from behind and put a choke hold on Chelsea throat. My mom screamed; "You black whore, you don't know who you're fucking with!! I'll kill you for touching my baby!!"

They rolled around on the floor with Chelsea trying to get loose,
but Ruth Ann had a death grip on Chelsea's neck from behind.

Chelsea started gasping for air, trying to say; "I can't breathe"!!

Mavis grabbed my mom's arm and tried to loosen her grip screaming,

"turn her loose! turn her loose! you're killing her!!!"

My mom Ruth Ann, finally loosen her grip and let Chelsea drop to the floor.

Chelsea lay on the floor and continued gasping for air.

Gradually, Chelsea began breathing normally again, but looked dazed.

But she was alright.

Corrina my girlfriend, grabbed Ruth Ann by the arm and led her outside to sit in the car, while I walked behind them. My mother Ruth Ann Hugged me crying, "are you alright baby"!

Corrina said;

"Chelsea has long had that coming, because she is a racist and a bully".

Inside the meeting place, the group was saying to Chelsea,

"maybe now you'll stop bullying people around".

Ms. Maldonado concluded the meeting by saying:

"This meeting is concluded, and I'll see you all at our next meeting next week".

CHAPTER 17

RELASPSE

Niqqie was not feeling good about herself after her mother ended up fighting Chelsea. She was disappointed after this first meeting with those whom she felt could understand what she was going through.

Ruth Ann was driving, but before they got to Niqqie's apartment, they stopped at a local fast food place to get a snack.

Standing near the door of the food place, was a pusher whom Niqqie and Corrina knew. They made eye contact with him.

Niqqie greeted him and he pushed a rock into Niqqie's hand and whispered, "call me".

Immediately Niqqie stop, put the rock in her purse and continued walking.

Ruth Ann was walking ahead, but Corrina saw what was happening between Niqqie and the pusher.

Corrina said quietly; "don't do it Niqqie, throw it away".

Ruth Ann was unaware of what had just happened.
When the rock touched Niqqie's hand, the anxiety of wanting to use again swept over

Niqqie's body.

After they finished eating Niqqie kissed her mom and said,

"Thank you mom for hanging with me, you guys go ahead. I'll walk home from here, I need the exercise".

Ruth Ann Responded;
"Okay, but be careful, "I'll leave my work phone number with Melba".
Ruth Ann said she would be talking to the social worker about her grandson.

Corrina Said, "can I talk with you for a minute Niqqie?".
They moved to the side of the car and Corrina whispered,

"I know what you are going to do Niqqie, and I beg you, please don't do it.
I have been down that road before, and I know what you are feeling.
Please get back in the car with us and let us take you home, please!"

Niqqie said; "I'll talk to you later Corrina. Thanks for everything".

As soon as Corrina and Ruth Ann drove off, Niqqie walked over to the car where the pusher was, and got in the back seat with him.

While locked in an embrace, Niqqie disappeared with him down in the back seat, as the car drove away. While Niqqie lay on her back in the back seat she pulled her dress up, pulled her underwear off, and opened her legs. When he saw her pussy, his dick immediately got hard.

He said, "you really want to fuck, don't you. Well I am going to give you what you want bitch", and pulled his pants down.

Niqqie said, "Yeah let's see what you've got". She guided his dick into her pussy.
When he pushed it in, Niqqie screamed, "You're too big, stop! stop!" But grabbed his butt cheeks and raised her legs to open them wider and began to screw.

Then he raised up and turned Niqqie over on her stomach. Niqqie thought he was going to enter her pussy from behind, but instead, he guided his big dick into her asshole and pushed.

Niqqie screamed; "it's in the wrong hole! It's in the wrong hole!" and tried to move out from under him, but he held her by her hips and kept pushing his dick in until her asshole got wet.

Then it got good to me, and I screwed him back. This was my first experience of being fucked in my ass hole. She closed her eyes and buried her head in the back seat cushion of the car but kept pushing her ass hole up to meet his thrust, moaning in pain and pleasure.

He said "You're mine now baby". He fucked me in ass until he filled my asshole with his cum. My ass hole kept opening and closing sucking his dick in until his dick got soft. I begged him not to stop and kept fucking him until he got off my back. I laid on my stomach for a while until the intense sexual sensation feeling subsided.

It was then and there that I said to myself,

"you're a fucking Nymphomaniac, bitch; you are addicted to fucking in any form! like the moderator said in the AA meeting!"

I became extremely angry with myself and wanted to die right then and there! Afterward, I made them stop at a gas station to allow me to use the restroom to clean myself up.

In the meantime Ruth Ann was trying to stay in touch with Kashi, her grandson. Ruth Ann contacted the Social Worker to inquire about Kashi. Carrie the Social worker told her that Kashi would have to placed in Foster Care soon, because he had stayed in the facility as long as he was allowed to.

She asked Ruth Ann if she was going to take Kashi if she was going to take Kashi to live with her.

Ruth Ann declined to accept custody of Kashi because, at the time, Ruth Ann could not care for the child properly; But, Ruth Ann continued to visit her grandchild regularly in the facility and to provide for some of his needs.

More than three months passed and Melba had not heard any word of Niqqie.

This time Melba had become worried, and decided to call Niqqie's mother, Ruth Ann. Ruth Ann didn't answer her phone, but Melba left a message on Ruth Ann's phone to call her.

Ruth Ann got the message and decided to go to melba's apartment, because she sensed something was wrong.

Ruth Ann arrived at Melba's apartment an hour later and got an update on Niqqie's disappearance. They decided to go to Niqqie's apartment.

Melba and Ruth Ann knocked on Niqqie's door, but there was no one answered.
So, Ruth Ann and Melba went to the manager and finally persuaded her to open Niqqie's door to see if she was in there.

Melba had expressed concern because Niqqie had said if She didn't get Kashi back she didn't want to live anymore.

They found Niqqie gone, thank God.

Ruth Ann and Melba went Back to the apartment to talk.

Ruth Ann asked Melba to please be honest with her and
Tell her everything. Melba agreed to tell all.

She began with how Charcoal and Flyboy the pusher first got Niqqie
Hooked on crack cocaine and marijuana.

Niqqie and Charcoal would argue over Charcoal staying out most of the night regularly, right after they got married.

The reason Charcoal gave for not taking her with him, was that he didn't want to kill nobody for trying to make it with her.

Melba admitted, "He sure would have to kill somebody, because that gal is a fine pretty little thing. I don't like to go nowhere with her either, she puts me to shame."

Melba told Ruth Ann how bad Charcoal would treat Niqqie on a daily routine. After he lost his job behind that crack cocaine, he would steal everything in sight, including the food out of his baby's mouth to buy more crack cocaine.

Ruth Ann offered her worldly wisdom by saying,
"I told Niqqie he was no good before she married him. I haven't found
a black man yet, that really know how to treat a woman. That's why I
don't mess with black men at all."

Melba shot back,
"Oh, and who are you messing with Ms. Ann,
Jesus Christ? White men are no better, all they want to do
is fuck you in the dark, and pay you off before it gets light, until the next time.
If white men are so much better, why didn't Niqqie's father marry you?
How many white families have you been introduced to, as the next Mrs. Stoneberg?
At least, Niqqie was married, and she is not pretending to be white either."

This straight forward attack shocked Ruth Ann. Nobody
had ever confronted her so harshly. But then, this was Ruth
Ann's first real encounter with real ghetto life.

She found out, it can be as much of a culture shock to blacks who think
they are above it all, as it is for white people.

Ruth Ann was taken aback for a moment, but just for a moment,
because Ruth Ann had her head together.

Ruth Ann turned slowly to have eye contact with Melba, and went
into her teaching mode.

(Ruth Ann is an excellent teacher, majoring in
English literature and with a Masters in Education Administration. She spoke with
perfect diction and deliberateness).

"What do you suggest I do, Melba, to prove that I'm black"? She waited for
a response, as a good teacher would do, although the question was rhetorical.
Ruth Ann wanted Melba to start thinking.

Ruth Ann then said,
"Should I act ignorant and boisterous with drugs or alcohol, using
ghetto language, or so called black English, cursing and fighting
and challenging my man, or all black men, for who is the
greatest? Or should I fall down and open my legs to every
black nigger who wants to fuck me? Maybe you think I should start using crack cocaine
to prove that I am just like every other black nigger woman addicted to drugs and
alcohol?"

Melba, was now thoroughly intimidated by the intellectual prowess of Ruth Ann, but said softly and in a question;

"You could have been a better mother"?

Ruth Ann dropped her head and said, "Touché,"

then broke down into uncontrolled sobbing.

Melba hugged her and cried with her. They both loved little Niqqie very much.

CHAPTER 18

NIQQIE DISAPPEARS

When the crying finally subsided, Melba finished telling Ruth Ann about
Niqqie's drug addiction, and the life style Niqqie had developed after being turned out
by Charcoal and Flyboy the pusher.

Ruth Ann voiced grave concern for her daughter and vowed to help her end her
addiction. But first they must find her.

Ruth Ann said she would start by talking to the social
worker about Kashi their young son. Ruth Ann gave her work phone number with
Melba.

Ruth Ann now, was not the same cool deliberate speaking schoolteacher,
Melba had come to know. Instead she was nervous and spoke rapidly.

Ruth Ann finally persuaded Melba to come with her to look for Niqqie.
Melba explained that since she was shot, she didn't visit those kinds of places
anymore, but she would go along for Niqqie's sake.

After about an hour of driving from one place to another,
Melba saw a girl who used to be with Niqqie sometimes. The
girl's name was Sandra.

She was what is known on the streets as a "strawberry."

That simply meant, she would do any kind of sexual act to get high.

Melba called Sandra over to the car.

Melba asked, "have you seen Niqqie?"

Sandra answered, "me and her, we don't run together no
more cause she got AIDS."

Ruth Ann screamed and fell over the steering wheel crying hysterically.

Sandra continued, "she may be in that old house on the corner where nobody lives.

Do you have a dollar you could let me have, I'm hungry."

Melba gave her a dollar and Sandra walked away.

Melba got Ruth Ann calm enough to drive to the end of the
block where the old house was. Melba got out walked up to the
door that was half opened, then turned around and came back
to the car.

She said to Ruth Ann, "I'm not going in there for anybody," and got back into the car.

They waited for awhile, and soon a man in disarranged
clothing came out and approached the car. Ruth Ann hit the
starter to drive off, but the man had his hand on the door.

He said to Melba, "I know you Melba, so, you decided you would finally

come looking for your lover man, Pinky, eh.

I bet you don't even recognize me, but I know you."

Melba looked at him and said, "Pinky, is that you? Boy, how are you doing, I haven't

seen you since," Pinky finished her statement, "yeah, your

accident."

Melba became serious with pinky and asked, "do you know

Niqqie and Charcoal."

Pinky said, "yeah I know them, what about them, who is that fine figure of a woman

over there, aren't you going to introduce me?"

Melba said, "that's Niqqie's mother, is Niqqie in there?"

"I don't know, she may be, what's it worth to you, ma'am?" he said, looking past Melba

at Ruth Ann. Ruth Ann reached in her pocket book and pulled out her little purse.

Melba stopped her hand and said, "go tell Niqqie to come out here and then we will

give you something."

Pinky took off running back into the house. Shortly, three

or four people came running out of the house.

Melba called out, "what's wrong?" A voice came back, "there is a lady dead in there." Melba and Ruth Ann jumped out of the car and started to enter the house.

"Just then, Pinky ran out, breathing very rapidly, and said, "I think Niqqie is dead, and nobody wants to be here when the police come. Can I have my money please? I've got to get out of here."

Ruth Ann started once again to enter the house. Pinky grabbed Ruth Ann's arm and said, "ma'am, I wouldn't go in there if I was you. Give me some money, I'll call the police."

Ruth Ann gave him a quarter and a five dollar bill and said, "please call the police."

Melba and Ruth Ann stood on the porch crying. Within minutes they heard the sirens. A crowd begins to gather. The police arrived and approached with drawn guns.

They cautiously walked upon the porch and told Ruth Ann and Melba to move back off the porch. The paramedics arrived and started to approach the house.

The police yelled, "stay back! stay back!" One officer stood on each side of the door and said, "this is the police, everybody inside come out with your hands up!"

A voice from the crowd yelled, "ain't nobody in there but the dead girl!" The police finally entered the house and called for the paramedics.

Shortly, the paramedics and the police came out of the house. Ruth Ann stood anxiously as the gurney was carefully moved down the steps. Then she saw it. Niqqie's face was not covered by the sheet.

Ruth Ann screamed, "she's not dead! My baby is not dead!"

Yes, little Niqqie was alive, barely. Melba was allowed to ride with Niqqie in the ambulance, while Ruth Ann drove behind them. They immediately took Niqqie into intensive care.

Ruth Ann rushed up to the gurney and tried to hug Niqqie.

The medical personnel said "move back lady if you want this girl to live, she's going fast."

"But, I'm her mother", cried Ruth Ann.

"I'm sorry ma'am, I didn't know. Please follow us inside the Hospital and go over to the desk, they will want to talk to you".

The nurse said softly, as she escorted Ruth Ann to the desk.

"Stay here, I'll be back".

The clerk placed some papers before Ruth Ann and said,

" Would you please fill out these documents to let us know who this young lady is and what your relationship to her is."

Hours seemed like days passed as Ruth Ann and Melba waited.

As they waited, they talked about their lives growing up, to the present.

Despite being miles apart intellectually, they had a lot in common.

After about four hours, a doctor came from the emergency intensive care section and was pointed to Ruth Ann by the nurse.

As the Doctor neared them, Ruth Ann grabbed the arm Of Melba and held on as the Oriental Doctor approached them.

"You two can relax now, "I am Doctor Soyo said the doctor,

"Monique is breathing normally now, but she is not out of the woods yet.

She is very weak from dehydration and lack of food. She has not spoken directly yet, and responds reluctantly. She still has some drugs and alcohol in her system and her heart is very weak. We have her on intravenous feeding for nourishment. We are now doing some tests to find out what caused her condition. When the results come back we will determine a treatment plan."

"Can we see her now?" Ruth Ann asked impatiently.

The Doctor said; "Well, She is not communicating sufficiently yet. I suggest you ladies go and get some rest and return during visiting hours.

We need some more time with her.

Its 2:00 A.M. now, and I know you must be tired.

So, visiting hours begin at 10:00 A.M. come back then"

The doctor started to leave.

Ruth Ann said, "Wait a minute doctor, have you done any blood test yet?"

The Doctor responded; "If you are asking what I think you are asking, we have been in touch with the health Department about her husband and we are preceding accordingly".

Ruth Ann began to cry again, as she asked the Doctor.

"Did she try to commit suicide?"

The Doctor said, "I would say from her reluctance to respond that she lost the desire to live and stopped eating. She doesn't seem to care a whole lot about living. We will know more when she talks to us. Now I really must go."

The doctor shook their hands before he walked away.

Melba remarked to Ruth Ann, "I am a little tired and I need to take my medicine".

Ruth Ann responded by taking Melba home, but said,

"I'm going to stay here at this hospital until my baby talks to me."

She asked Melba to call Charcoal's mother and father

and tell them what had happened to Niqqie. Melba

promised she would try to get the number because she had lost

Charcoal's mother's number.

Ruth Ann returned to the hospital and finally fell asleep on

the couch in the lobby.

"Ms. Nasareth, Ms. Nasareth, Ms. Nasareth, wake up, Ms. Nasareth,

I would like to talk to you."

Finally the nurse was able to wake Ruth Ann. "Ms. Nazareth,

I'm going off shift now, but before I leave, I wanted to bring you

up to date on Monique's condition. She is still very weak from pneumonia

attack, and from a lack of nourishment.

She is still refusing to eat or talk to anyone.

We are continuing to feeding her intravenously. She shakes her head negatively

whenever we tell her you want to see her. Sometimes a parent is able

to help us under such circumstances, but we have hesitated to bring you in, because

Monique seems to not want to see you. Is there anything you

can tell us that may help us to get her to cooperate?"

"Well, I love Monique, although I may not have shown it
under circumstances when it was crucial for her to know.

CHAPTER 19

NIQQIE'S HOSPITALIZATION

Nonetheless, her not wanting to see me hurts me deeply. That
in itself tells me that whatever happened between us is at least
partly to blame for her present condition. We grew up very close,
and at times we only had each other. Whenever she would
become obstinate in times past, it appeared that all she wanted
was to make me prove that I loved her, by some act of affection,
such as a hug and a kiss. Perhaps if I could just say a word to
her, she might respond."

"I agree with you Ms. Nazareth", the nurse responded,
"that's why I suggested to the doctor to allow you to come
in, despite what Monique indicates. I know the kind of bond
a mother and daughter form under such circumstances.
I too am raising a daughter without a father."

Ruth Ann spoke very softly,
"would you mind calling me Ruth Ann?"

"No not at all, and you can call me Peggy," the
nurse responded.

"Come with me Ruth Ann."

As they walked down the long corridor, Peggy continued to talk;
"We have moved Monique into what we call isolation, do you understand
what that means Ruth Ann?"

Ruth Ann nodded in agreement.

The nurse continued, "What that means is, we
think Monique may have been in contact with a contagious virus
from her husband, the AIDS virus. Does that frighten you Annie?"

Tears begin to well up in Annie's eyes as she slowed her
pace to a stop and turned her face to the wall of the corridor.
She began to sob softly in a trembling motion. The nurse put her arms around Ruth
Ann's shoulders and said softly.
"I wanted you to know this before we went into Monique's room.
Monique doesn't look very good now and I didn't want you to
break up when you see her. You do know about the AIDS possibility, don't you?"

"Not very much", Ruth Ann replied.

"come over here and sit down." Peggy directed her to a seating area just outside of the
isolation ward where the over garments and masks are kept for visitors.

"I'm going to get the Doctor to talk with you."

Peggy returned shortly with Monique's doctor.

"This is Ruth Ann, Monique's mother. I don't believe Ms. Nasareth

has been appraised of her daughter's complete condition".

"How do you do Ms. Nazareth's, I am Doctor Solisbeth ", the doctor said as he

sat down beside her.

"I'll start from the beginning.

About two months ago, Monique's husband, Malcolm Jacob, street name Charcoal; Is

that is your daughter's husband's name?"

Ruth Ann answered, " I think it is?"

The Doctor said, " not maybe or, I think so. I need a positive answer from you Ms.

Nazareth of, yes or no. Is that the name of your daughter's husband?

Ruth Ann answered, "yes".

The doctor said: "Thank You Ms. Nazareth. He was arrested for possession of drugs

and paraphernalia. The police had been called, because he was

standing outside a store trying to solicit money from one of the

store's customers.

Apparently, he had got pretty obstinate with

the owner when he was told to move on. So, the owner called the police.

When the police arrived, they found him somewhat delirious, talking about seeing things, about fighting off monsters that was trying to eat his flesh, and poking holes in

his head. They brought him here, to the Psych jail ward, where extensive tests

were done, and he indeed tested positive for HIV in the third stage which meant

that he had aids.

Before he was discharged to a hospice, he gave the names of all the ones he

could remember whom had had sex with him in the last year.

Of course his wife Monique, known as Niqqie your daughter, was number one on the

list.

The health department set out to locate these people. So, we were happy to

have Monique brought in to us.

Before you ask any more questions, let me say this,

Monique has not yet shown the primary symptoms of having the AIDS virus

so far. She is sick because she was slowly dying from dehydration and lack of food.

She is presently being detoxed to get all the drugs and alcohol out of her system.

However, there are psychological indications, that her condition is the result of a not so

subtle attempt at suicide.

Any questions"?

Ruth Ann asked the Doctor "Where is Charcoal, Monique's husband, now?"

The Doctor replied, "I think he was given only about four months to live. He was discharged to a hospice and I don't know where that is at this time.

Now I must go. We will have a chance to talk later, Peggy, she is all yours".

Ruth Ann, now completely composed said, "may I go in to see my daughter now?"

Nurse Peggy answered, "yes ma'am, right through that door".

The doctor and the nurse lingered behind a bit to see Ruth Ann enter Niqqie's room.

When Ruth Ann entered her daughter's room and stood beside Niqqie's bed, she observed the covers were pulled up tight around her shoulders, so that only Niqqie's neck and head were visible.

Ruth Ann stood and stared at the boney facial features once housing a face that could have won any beauty contest. Now the flesh sagged around the boney face structure as though the face had been deflated. The big dark brown almond shaped eyes with the tantalizing glance, stared blankly from a pool of dark circles. Tears rolled gently down the well kept cheeks of Ruth Ann, but never marring her natural beauty, as her eyes locked into Niqqie's eyes.

Slowly Ruth Ann moved closer to Niqqie's side of the bed. Ruth Ann's right hand moved over the sheets until it reached the face of her daughter and gently touched the soft face of Niqqie her daughter.

Niqqie's eyes moistened while her sagging facial muscles strained to hold back the tears.

Finally Niqqie's face begins to convulse as the sobs accelerated into a mournful cry.

Then Ruth Ann broke down into a full cry as her arms swooped down to fully embrace her child.

They spoke at the same time as if they had rehearsed it. "Forgive me, baby." "Forgive me, mama."

Nurse Peggy, a very beautiful Pilipino girl with olive skin tone, and the doctor slowly backed out the door as Ruth Ann and little Niqqie locked themselves around each other rocking back and forth.

"You are a real nurse, aren't you, Peggy? said the Doctor, "You should have been off more than two hours ago."

Peggy responded, "But for the grace of God, there go I," as she pointed toward Ruth Ann. "I have a young daughter, too, that I'm raising without the benefit of her father."

END

CHAPTER 20

Epilogue and Analogy of Novel IN RYHME & METER

<u>Boys and girls need a father figure</u>

What will a child amount to without good direction?

If an eagle is not taught to fly, will it rule the skies?

A child's behavior may well be that refection.

And when a pig is haltered, is it not being readied to be sliced like a pie?

With the pieces being laid out like tile

Any child when incarcerated is overly exposed to badness.

Such a child can be a cause for society's sadness.

No Way To Win

I have often wondered about what's going on inside my
head.

It is a constant war, and it's the outcome I have come to
dread.

My friend obeyed the bad voice, and in time he turned up
dead.

Another one obeyed the good voice, and ended up sick in
bed.

Sometimes, what I do, I think will surely make me shine.

When things go right, unforeseen circumstances turn them around.

Do what's right, and forget the outcome, is advice that is sound.

For time is the only constant thing, don't forget, God is not blind.

RESEARCH ANALYSIS

THE STORYLINE of this novel, of child abuse, substance addiction and sex addiction is nothing new to the world.

All three have long been a problem among black Americans and for society as a whole. Drugs such as tobacco, alcohol, marijuana are said to be gateway drugs to the use hard drugs such as cocaine, crack cocaine, crystal meth, hereon. These hard drugs appear to displace the natural pleasure principle in the mind, which completes the natural emotion of love.

Opiates, alcohol, cocaine and other drugs known since the beginning of human history have long been used to transport it's users to another state of mind for various reasons.

The introduction and use of crack cocaine and crystal meth however, has added another dimension to the substance addiction cycle. It appears that crack or meth can seize control of the mind the first time it is used. This novel emphasizes the lack of concern for others by those addicts using addictive drugs.

Intense sexual feelings, accentuated by such drugs may drive one to prostitution; thus, may be used as a means to maintain drug addiction.

Whereas, sex addiction in women may be known clinically as Nymphomania (the uncontrollable desire to have sex), could be seen as a mental disorder that may be diagnosed as an addiction that may not be accompanied by drug use.

Nonetheless, sex addiction may be diagnosed among gay and lesbian people and may become a prominent fixture among some in the gay and lesbian community.

Sex addiction nonetheless, in most cases, may go hand in hand with drug addiction and finances from such addiction may be used to support the drug addiction.

All the above being a withstanding theory of this Author, such drugs of choice appears to disconnect the aspect of the created emotional human "love" from the created instinctual aspect of sexual attraction that God reserved for use to populate the earth with humankind.

The sexual act itself, as seen in instinctive sex relations between lower animals, proves that the sex act itself, is a Godly creation.

Such disconnect from the Godly created emotion of love itself, by drug addicts and sex addicts, appear to allow humans to engage in the sexual act by itself without the pre-disposition of the emotional "love" created by God.

The source of sex acts engaged in by drug and sex addicts appear more instinctual, like lower animals. In theory, some cases of drug and sex addiction; **incest**, or sex between blood relatives may easily occur as a result.

My research indicates that once a person actually gets high the first time from such drugs, he or she may enter the first stage of the addiction cycle.

The cycle runs for four stages.

I have named "4 Stages of Denial." These stages are titled and are cited here but explained in my first book, **"THE ADDICTIVE BEHAVIORAL PERSONALITY, OUT OF CONTROL".**

DRUG ADDICTION CYCLE:

Stage 1. DENIAL THAT HE OR SHE HAS A PROBLEM.

Stage 2. DENIAL THAT THEIR USE OF DRUG OF CHOICE IS THE CAUSE

OF PROBLEMS.

Stage 3. DENIAL OF DRUG BEHAVIOR IS CAUSING PROBLEMS FOR OTHERS.

Stage 4. DENIAL THAT HE OR SHE IS HELPLESS IN CONTROLLING USE

OF DRUG UNTIL THE ADDICT CRASH, OR DIES, OR TRIGGERS

UNINTENTIAL SUICIDE.

When the addiction cycle is triggered, the person is addicted; **WHICH MEANS THAT THE ADDICT FEELS THAT THEY MUST CONTINUALLY USE THE DRUG OF CHOICE IN ORDER TO REMAIN FUNCTIONABLE,** and is destined to reach a point of no return. Such a point of no return **MEANS THAT THE ADDICT FEELS THAT THEY CAN NEVER BE THE SAME WITHOUT THE USE OF THE DRUG OF CHOICE.** This means that the addict may lose the will to live and may end their life with involuntary suicide, or outright suicide. My **observational research** indicates that the addict cannot end the cycle. The addiction cycle must run its course by natural means.

In many cases, some addicts have found the fortitude to try and end the addiction cycle on their own if they can muster up the psychological tools **from within themselves.** Those who have been able to stop using the drug of choice and remain drug free on their own have told me, that their parental training of the work ethic and the teaching of the A, B, C, of life, early in their childhood, have been instrumental in retooling their resistance.

Nonetheless, **all too many have continued in a, so called, self control addiction cycle and have ended up inhabiting the so called, "Skid row" areas, of the big cities of the world.**

****

But first, How did Kashi's parents get into such a dilemma?

It seems clear that Niggie and Charcoal have developed an addiction personality of both sex addiction and drug addiction.

The development of the Addictive Behavioral Personality can be traced back to early childhood. It is usually developed in the home, or wherever the child spends the beginning of his or her life through adolescence.

The addictive personality should be defined this way:
Symptoms of needing to make some kinds of behavior habitual
or ritualistic, in order to function in a state of normalcy in society.

This developmental mode of behavior for the development of a addiction personality is usually due to feelings of inadequacy, or guilt, or anger, or all three usually cause by dysfunction in the family.

The addictive personality therefore is a defensive maneuver by the mind to offset ego

167

conflict.

It is interesting to note, my research indicates a lifelong addictive personality can start to be developed at any interval during the time period of birth through adolescence; but not after adolescence.

Niqqie's son Kashi has been set up to develop an addictive personality very early after birth, just like his father.

.

Please keep in mind that even though addictive scenarios may be operative in the child's home during these early years, it does not mean the child will develop a lifelong addictive pattern.

I believe, what I call the unknown entity (unconscious self contained energy source of collected thought patterns and, spiritual connection in a child) that is present from birth, with what Freud calls the Id (unconscious basic instincts instilled from birth) cooperate to form the basis for an identifiable personality.

That being so, I believe the developing of an addictive personality can be influenced pro or con, by the unknown entity, if it wants to, by way of the superego.

I will talk more about the psychological aspect of the Super-ego.

On the other hand; if that unknown entity is addictively orientated innately (born), **the person will develop an addictive personality,** despite the absence of addictive scenarios in the home during childhood.

SEX ADDICTION

In many cases when treating drug addiction, it is found those persons may be addicted to sex also, either heterosexually, or homosexually.

Supported by my scholarly approach, other research techniques, deductive reasoning, content analysis, plus some empirical evidence; I believe any predisposition for overactive sexual behavior and sexual feelings toward the same sex is also influenced during the uniting of the female egg and male sperm in the womb.

I find there is some evidence to support homosexuality, in some cases, to start developing when the birth cells combine to form the embryo. (according to the genetic findings of the Scientist Fraud).

Notwithstanding, genetics, and or a very strong predisposition from the unknown entity toward overactive sexual behavior of any sort, may support the idea of psychological homosexual feelings from birth.

But to become an actual lifelong homosexual, (I believe a lot of evidence will support my conclusions), **still remains a matter of choice.**

There is some empirical evidence, and I do believe this also, that homosexual feelings in some cases are uncontrollable by the person; albeit **unaccepted** as **natural or normal behavior,** in the specific meaning of those two terms in America or society as a whole.

The pre-occupation with sexual behavior of any sort in early childhood, provides an addictive scenario that may lead to the use of addictive drugs.

Conversely, early addictive drug behavior may predispose a person to overactive sexual behavior of any sort.

It is reported by all addicts that spoke about sex addiction, that drugs such as, crack, cocaine is a sexually active drug.

If an addict has latent homosexual or extreme sexual tendencies toward sexual behavior of any sort, such as rape, pedophile, sexual torture, or sexual murder; some drugs may bring them out of the closet.

Nevertheless, sex stimulation as well as sex addiction precipitated by the drug of choice is demonstrated in most addicts.

REFRENCES:

Calhoun, M. (C)2014); Men And Women and Change, Chapter 27

"Strange case of a he-man", p163-168

Calhoun, Moses (C)1993) The *Addictive Behavioral Personality, Out Of Control,*

Chapter 8 "Addictive Scenarios", (p149-168)

Levin, Jerome D. (C)1987) THE TREATMENT OF ALCOHOLISM AND OTHER

ADDICTIONS ,"Dynamics of Drug Addiction" (p194-197)

www.ingramcontent.com/pod-product-compliance
Lightning Source LLC
Chambersburg PA
CBHW030015290326
41934CB00005B/349